UNCHAINED
A VOICE APART

MATTHEW MAHER

UNCHAINED: A VOICE APART
Copyright © 2018 by Matthew Maher. All rights reserved.

Edited by Cherri Olsen

This title is also available as a 55:11 Publishing product.
Visit www.5511publishing.com for more information.

Unless otherwise indicated, all materials on these pages are copyrighted by Matthew Maher. All rights reserved. No part of this publication may be reproduced, stored in an information or retrieval system, or transmitted in any way by any means, electronic, mechanical, photocopy, recording, or otherwise without the prior permission of the Publisher, except as provided by USA copyright law.

Unless otherwise noted, all Scripture quotations are taken from the New King James Version of the Bible (Public Domain).
Published by 55:11 Publishing LLC

1701 Walnut Street 7th Floor | Philadelphia, Pennsylvania 19103 USA
info@5511publishing.com | www.5511publishing.com

55:11 Publishing is committed to Publishing with Purpose. The company reflects the philosophy established by the founders, based on Isaiah 55:11: "So is My word that goes out from My mouth; it will not return to Me empty, but will accomplish what I desire and achieve the purpose for which I sent it."

Book design copyright © 2018 by
5511 Publishing LLC. All rights reserved.

Cover design by Tim Janicki, Sight2Site Media, www.s2smedia.net

Published in the United States of America

ISBN: 978-0-9986306-2-5

Acknowledgements

I would like to place Jesus Christ, my Lord and Savior, on the throne of this book. Meaning, without His Lordship, there is no power or purpose in my authorship. In addition, without the unwavering support and influence of my sweet wife, Sarah, I would not have the mood, motivation, or margin to engage the calling of ministry.

I would also like to thank the Cape May County Herald, especially its owners, Art and Patricia Hall, for presenting me the platform of *Prison Talk* as the manifestation of a confined voice and also my post prison platform of *#iCONVICTION* and its subsequent replacement, *Truth Over Trend*. Because of your faith believing in my faith, together we were blessed to be able to inspire other people's faith. And now, your spark has set this book ablaze.

Lastly, but not entirely, I would like to gratefully acknowledge Mrs. Cherri Olsen for her ministry of editing. Without her assistance, none of my thoughts would have been graciously seasoned with salt.

Thank you, the reader and community, also.

In memory of Hort Kap.

Contents

Acknowledgements, *iii*

Introduction, 1

1. My True Release Date, 9
2. I Have More Than Most, 12
3. A Day in the Life, 15
4. Choosing to Get Up, 19
5. Gifts in the Storm, 22
6. Why Waste the Pain?, 25
7. Seeking Approval, 28
8. The Rose of Confidence, 30
9. Envision Your Future, 33
10. Savoring Every Breath, 36
11. To My Father, 39
12. What Have I Done?, 41
13. August Tears, 44
14. Can You Hear Me Now?, 47
15. My Position of Passion, 50
16. A View Apart (How One Views the Time), 53
17. God Sees the Heart, 56
18. The Birth of New Life, 59
19. Scars Tell a Story, 62

CONTENTS

20. The Man in the Mirror, 65
21. Cloud 9, 68
22. The Telling of a Tear, 71
23. Faces Frozen in Time, 74
24. Light From Darkness, 77
25. Well Traveled, 80
26. The Reality of Faith, 83
27. How Well You Show, 86
28. Polarized Degrees, 88
29. Alivia's Eye's of Hope, 91
30. A Few Years Ago, 94
31. Tragedy Warrants a Response, 97
32. What Matters Most, 99
33. I Wonder, 102
34. Nowhere to Go but Up, 105
35. My Final Talk From Prison, 107
36. Holiday Musing, 110
37. The #iCONVICTION Movement, 115
38. Out of Perspective Pain, 118
39. Formative Years || Formative Prayers, 120
40. The Essence of a Father, 122
41. Set Backs Can Be Set Ups, 125
42. A Place of Projection, 128
43. This Present Comfort, 130
44. The Triumph of Trouble, 132
45. The Disconnection of Connection, 135

46. Walking in God-Opened Doors, 138
47. Setting the Tone, 141
48. Reflect and Reality Check, 144
49. The Answer to the World's Confusion, 147
50. Failures Aren't the End, 150
51. Living in Today's Trust, 153
52. Now That's a Swan Song, 155
53. Getting a Hold on Sorrow, 158
54. Example Trumps Verbal, 161
55. Success of the Soul, 164
56: Standing Strong, 167
57. Sharing the Breath of God, 170
58. Take Advantage of the Dash, 172
59. Hold Your Peace, 175
60. My Dead Hands, 178
61. Isolated Decisions, 181
Conclusion, 183

About the Author, 187
About the CORE CONVICTION SERIES, 189
Connect with Matthew Maher, 190
Also available from Matthew Maher, 191
If you enjoyed this book…, 193

Introduction

At the time a majority of the words in this book were penned, I had spent many years going no further than 100 yards in a prison yard; yet my voice had somehow managed to reach around the world. You see, while I was chained by my consequences, I was *Unchained* in conscience and liberated through the Word of God.

This compilation is a series of columns that I wrote from behind the wall for a newspaper in the community that I had once resided. These thoughts are truly the manifestation of a confined voice.

Like the Apostle Paul, who wrote some of his epistles from prison, God had graced me with this platform to write a column from prison. Remarkable from every standard of the Word, in spite of your preference of faith. Not because I'm the author, but because I recognize Jesus as the Author and Finisher of my faith and this book, and it has only been made possible by my faith in Him and His grace on me.

I do not deserve it, but I have learned to promote it.

The writings represent precisely the evidence of the power of God's Word—*for which I am suffering even to the point of being chained like a criminal. But God's Word is not chained* (2 Timothy 2:9)—no matter the circumstances. They were written in real time, hard circumstances, and in a dark abysmal environment.

During my time locked up, I was held within the same restricted vicinity. It's as if there was an invisible chain around my ankle that kept me from going beyond the perimeter set for my captivity. Physically. But there is another aspect of my chain that had me leaping over those walls.

And that is why I desire with all my heart to share freedom: Because I know the chained feel of confinement.

For almost five years, I was content with a chained pattern of movements—tier to mess...tier to yard...tier to church...tier to visit hall, and reverse of these patterns—because I was spiritually free in those movements. Physically obedient to its limitations, while remaining mentally and spiritually obedient to liberation.

I don't yank my chain, but I've learned contentedness through its squeeze.

Conversely, I think about a dog that is chained to a pole, who sits anxiously waiting for his owner to free him. Yet after an extended period of time and continually being yanked back by the chain's restrictions and his impatience, he settles into his limitations. By force nonetheless.

Until one day, the owner releases the dog from his chain, but instead of going free, he remains close to the pole. Conformed to his boundaries. Staying by the pole has become his reality and as a result he is confined more than ever because of the mind's contortion. Twisted by captivity.

May it never be.

May we never get so locked in to a choke hold that we lose our voice forever.

One of the main controversial questions that people have asked me while confined, and now while free, is *"Why do you think you deserve a voice?"* My response has been one and the same from the very beginning. I humbly reply, "I did not ask for a voice, not then and not now, it was presented to me." And to be honest, I don't deserve a voice, but the recipients of the messages do—those who read the columns then and to whomever finds their way to these pages now.

You see, silencing a "Public Service Announcement" (PSA) is failing to agree with the service of the public. I wonder which voice is more of a detriment to society: The one that owns up to his negative in order for others to do positive? Or the one that negates the positive because they'd rather focus on the negative? Hmmm…

Demonstrating accountability and owning up to our mistakes should be encouraged, not splintered. Any voice that is willing to provoke proper perspective ought not be provoked itself by those unwilling to promote anything but themselves. Their opinions. Their objections. Their conjectures.

I apologize, but this talk from the abyss of "prison" is raw at times. It must be due to the gross error, the misjudgment, and the tragedy that demands it.

Besides, and especially as I compile these writings now on the other side of confinement—in freedom, I realize that I did not have a voice, but the voice had me. *A Voice Apart*.

You cannot selfishly possess something when you know it has a greater purpose than you. You can only allow the greater to lead you. You can only shoulder it, which isn't you pressing up on it, but it pressing down on you.

It would have been a tragic shame if I allowed the *Voice* to fall on a muted tongue. You see, I had to agree with my circumstances at every juncture of this journey because the circumstances had me—mind, heart, and soul. These circumstances had me at *"brace yourself Matthew. The other driver is deceased!"* Words from the State Police Officer several hours after the motor vehicle collision I was responsible for; words that have fallen perpetually on my soul, and have moved me into a whole new role.

Not a role model as I once was—professional soccer player—but a role that made me the model to cautiously avoid, a mistake to receptively heed. The model however is only as impacting as the voice. The *Voice* in question was the sole work of the Holy Spirit's guidance, conviction, and discernment in my life. This voice apart became the mission of my heart. And God in His awesome power used the weak to confound the wise.

When I was released from prison, countless people from all walks of life approached me to say how much my column meant to them in their life circumstances. Can you imagine that? Words from the abyss shining light on other people's dark nights.

And it is for that reason that I pray these timeless themes inspire your conscience in the Lord and instigate your conviction for the Lord. Never forget that no matter what it is you are currently going through in this world of hurts, it is possible to be *Unchained* because of the Word in your heart.

"How can a young man cleanse his way? By taking heed according to Your word. With my whole heart I have sought You; Oh, let me not wander from Your commandments! Your word I have hidden in my heart, that I might not sin against You"
(Psalm 119:9-11).

UNCHAINED
A VOICE APART

1. My True Release Date

Jan. 7, 2010. That particular date—my sentencing day—will always elicit a floodgate of emotions. It is the day I received my five-and-a-half-year sentence, along with the unexpected blessing of a release date, a gift I could never deserve in a million years. One million words cannot properly describe this one date—one I will always remember—not for one million tears, but for one freeing hug.

I slept well on the eve of my sentencing, something that can only be attributed to the prayers of family, friends and countless others. I knew I was going to prison—something I still couldn't wrap my mind around. I used to watch the TV series *Prison Break* from the safety and comfort of my living room, never once imagining myself walking prison halls, or living a prison reality.

I woke up on Jan. 7, 2010 with feelings of uncertainty, but this was not a day to wrestle my fate. This was a day to face the family and loved ones of my innocent victim, Mr. Hort Kap.

I remember getting ready, the whole time imagining this day from their perspective. How would I feel facing the man who killed my father, brother, uncle, friend, or grandfather?

My heart was heavy as I rode to court that day, not preoccupied with what the prosecutor, judge, or public thought about me, but solely focused on the Kap family—their pain, their loss, and what they thought of me. And although I entered the courtroom knowing that in a matter of hours, I would be riding to prison, my new home for the next five, maybe 10 years, my mind was far from the calendar.

> The prospect of serving my time actually provided momentary relief, even if it was a mere grain of redemption buried beneath mountains of devastation—all caused by me.

The prospect of serving my time actually provided momentary relief, even if it was a mere grain of redemption buried beneath mountains of devastation—all caused by me. But it was a chance for me to begin to give back, trusting God's promise to *"work all things together for good, for those who love God, and who are called according to His purpose"* (Romans 8:28).

Nothing can bring Mr. Kap back, and nothing will ever diminish the unrelenting throb of a broken heart mourning a life senselessly lost. So I can only pray for healing and do my best to honor the life of the man I killed when I chose to drink and drive on March 7, 2009. I may very well deserve to sit alone

1. MY TRUE RELEASE DATE

in a prison cell for one million years, and if that were the case, I would still have that one hug, that one measure of peace, and that one release date. Knowing I was completely to blame for someone's death is my life sentence, and whether caged or free, that disgusting feeling will haunt me always.

I understand why nothing will ever be good enough for a million critics, and for that I am sorry. But I also know that when all is said and done, there is only One I must answer to—One judge, and One God—and where the spirit of the Lord is, there is liberty—whether caged, or free.

People still ask me for my release date, and my answer will always be Jan. 7, 2010—my true release date—granted in the form of an undeserved hug of forgiveness from Kap's oldest son, Noun. Jan. 7, 2010 will always be the day that one hug removed the weight of the world from my shoulders, and eased the burden I planned to carry with me to my grave. I stared at their pain that day in court, and their faces, expecting hatred to glare right back at me. But instead I saw the face and tears of selfless mercy, and felt the embrace of supernatural grace.

I am humbled to have this release date; one million writings will never be able to proclaim the peace granted through just one hug. God's grace to my case: one million to one!

2. I Have More Than Most

What's prison like? People who write me often want to know and prior to January 7, 2010, my first day here, I wondered the same thing. Well, let's see if I can describe it—at least the physical aspects of my environment. I will save the emotional aspects for another day. One thing is for sure, words cannot accurately paint a picture of prison, this place I now call home.

I am confined in a garage-like, dormitory setting with 38 men packed in like sardines. Everything is metal—trunks, bunks, lockers, tables, and the tiny, lone window on the back wall. The walls are cinder block—dented faces painted grey many times over, bordered by rust and old pipes. It is a boiler room without the boiler.

I sleep on a "prison pillow," thin and narrow, on a bunk equipped with a one-inch foam mattress wrapped in plastic. The air is stale, and the thick stench of cigarette smoke mixed with body odor moves through the tier courtesy of an oversized utility fan suspended from the ceiling. Nauseating isn't the

2. I HAVE MORE THAN MOST

right word. In the winter it's freezing; in the summer, hot like a sauna with temperatures climbing to over 117 degrees.

> My surroundings are all I have, but with God, I have more than most.

I brush my teeth with a tiny piece of plastic, about two inches long, and shave with a singular blade about the same size. And to think I used to complain about my Mach3 razor! There is one small, cloudy mirror in our bathroom. There are no light switches. Lights come on automatically at the crack of dawn and shut off by ten-thirty at night.

I live on the bare minimum, but this minimum has become my norm. I spend countless hours a day sitting in my green plastic chair working on projects for my future, reading and writing, leading a Bible study, and corresponding with friends and family. My own personal living area consists of a 6' by 8' living space, 3 of those feet are occupied by my bed. The toilet bowl is steel, the sanitation revolting. Shower and bathroom privacy, NONE! I was just thinking the other day that I haven't felt carpet under my feet in almost two years. Little things that I used to take for granted like music, silence, or fresh air, are considered luxuries here.

But this is the life of my doing. One night, one poor decision, an innocent life lost. No excuses. No complaints. I am paying the price for my reckless decision to drink and drive, even though that price can never commensurate the permanence of a lost life. I have purposed to honor the name of my victim, Mr. Hort Kap, in all that I do from here on out. But even so, it's not enough.

It will never be enough.

Today is all I have, tomorrow doesn't exist—that's how I approach each new day here in prison. The judge gave me one day at a time for five and a half years and I make the most of every day.

This will pass, all things eventually do, and my only prayer is that God will take my disaster and bring good from it. Comfortable it is not, but my mind has been at total peace since day one. I may be confined, but my spirit is not. Dusty floors, dirty walls, grimy gates, but because of my faith and reliance on God, I am content, at peace, and fully free.

To say that I am grateful for what God has done in my life is an understatement. I killed a man and deserve to pay with my own life. But God has shown mercy to me, and has given me hope in the midst of the darkness here. My surroundings are all I have, but with God, I have more than most.

3. A Day in the Life

A day in confinement can be viewed differently from the eyes of faith. What I have come to experience, despite much chaos and tension, is a peace that starts inwardly and hopefully is visible outwardly. In prison, the structure is so rigid, the routine so predictable, that you can easily become complacent. When I first arrived here, I had this eerie feeling that I was stuck in a never-ending "Ground Hog's Day." I'll try to give you a snapshot of a day, as this is my "true view" from here:

5:35 A.M. Only two other inmates are awake on the tier besides me. One is in the bathroom shaving and the other is drawing. The one drawing appears to have never gone to sleep. Lights will shoot on in 20 minutes and awaken only a few more. Around 6:10 A.M., the CO's loud demand to "count up" will act as a free man's alarm clock, only without the snooze button.

5:53 A.M. I've completed my core workout and daily devotions and my prayer time is next. I typically finish these things before 6:30 A.M. mess call. In spite of the depressing surroundings, I deliberately begin each day with thankfulness. I concluded my prayers with a line from the Prayer of Jabez, *"That I may cause no more pain."* I am strengthened by a passage in my Streams devotional, *"There is never a majestic mountain without a deep valley, and there is never a birth without pain."*

6:16 A.M. "Count Up" came and went and I am getting ready to do more reading and writing. Many inmates are beginning to stir for breakfast, and I watch from my green plastic chair as the chaos continues to rule the moment. Sadly, the majority of the inmates only get out of bed each day to be fed. I cannot imagine viewing this environment through faithless eyes.

6:30 A.M. A sharp, yet familiar, "Count is clear!" is announced over the PA system, meaning all inmates are present. Confinement at its finest. And although there is nothing "fine" about any of this, my eyes of faith uncover a valuable lesson in every view. It's now 8:10 A.M. and I'm wrapping up my reading and writing for now. I work as a teacher's assistant and I have to be upstairs in 20 minutes. Many believe working in prison is just a waste of time, but I am convinced that I must not allow this time to go to waste.

11:30 A.M. Lunch mess is called and it's the same scene as morning mess: many are asleep, some stir, and others are rushing towards the locked gate. Just more controlled chaos and noise.

1:20 P.M. I am back on the unit. I got called down from work to get legal mail. Legal mail to an inmate is always a downer as it reminds us of the pain we caused. Some respond selfishly, others with deep remorse; it just depends on your view. I choose to pray about my mail. I ask God for the wisdom to handle what-

> There is never a majestic mountain without a deep valley, and there is never a birth without pain.

ever needs handling, and for strength to release that which I have no control over. I refuse to allow negativity to creep into my life. It's all about weathering the moments as opposed to letting the storm brew for the day.

Time to write some letters; mail is consistent, so I must be too.

4:20 P.M. Dinner movement has livened the dead from their slumber and now things are really hopping! There are two card games going, the TV is blasting, obscenities are flowing, and rowdy nonsense fills the air. Many are conversing, but not casually. After dinner, depending on the weather, the pandemonium will continue in the yard. I usually just keep it moving and no more competition for me. In prison, a competition has no winner. If you win and the loser doesn't like it, he will make you lose (and I'm not talking about a rematch).

I learned this the hard way when I first got here. Sports and competition are my background, and many times I "played for fun," only to find out much later that my competitive spirit almost got me killed. The underlying rule here in prison is "compete at your own risk," where the risk could be your life, freedom, future or anything in between.

So for now, I just "keep it moving," (prison slang for interacting with all social groups), which is basically what I've been doing my entire life anyway. This is how I've been able to get to know so many people here, not to mention stay alive and healthy.

8:20 P.M. Back on the tier, rec was good and "safe." From my bunk, I observe this "zoo" in all its glory. I see lots of bodies, all dressed alike, but what exactly is being done? I see no purpose, no productivity, no peace. I hear lots of shouting and competing voices, yet what is being said? (Nothing worth repeating. Trust me). A fellow inmate just grumbled to another, "This is such a waste of time, isn't it?" I think, "No, you're wasting your time."

11 P.M. I am up later than usual. The lights are now out, so I'm writing under a miniature light. The TV is off, but the chaos lives on. Yet lying here on my bunk, settled (and sleepy) in the midst of this crazy storm, I cannot help but feel blessed. I'm so grateful for these eyes of faith and the perspective my "true view" offers.

4. Choosing to Get Up

It's been a rough few days, but I've regained my composure. I allowed a trivial incident to steal my peace and in so doing, learned that my peace can only be stripped from me if I let go of it myself. This week, I've felt myself slipping, my moods wavering, and my tolerance level at an all-time low. The constant chaos is trying at times—there is never a quiet moment and a lot of the time pure ignorance rules the environment. I feel like I am constantly pulled in a thousand directions, always trying to help and never wanting to disappoint. But this time, I allowed my circumstances to get the best of me instead of getting the best out of my circumstances.

I have to remember some distinct biblical principles when I'm feeling agitated—ones that apply whether on the outside or in this pit of darkness. First, salt should not lose its flavor, but

> **I firmly believe that faith that has not been tested cannot be trusted.**

add flavor. Second, light does not succumb to darkness, it overcomes darkness. I am supposed to be the "salt" and "light" in here, but have missed the opportunity lately. So now it's time to get up again. It's a new day with new opportunities. I'm beginning to realize that God's peace is something I should never grip loosely. After all, how can I expect to share so willingly something I can lose so easily? I must hold on tighter!

Thankfully, my faith has taught me that it doesn't matter if you fall, but whether or not you choose to get up again. It is like the difference between a sheep and a pig upon falling into a ditch. The sheep immediately works to get out, while the pig simply wallows in the mud. The sheep experiences discomfort after falling and focuses its energy on getting up, while the pig becomes comfortable in the dirt, settling into its new pen.

Comfort can be a curse in our lives. It was in mine. I had it all—the good life. I rarely focused my mind on things above, but actually preferred complacency—living for the day, going through the motions, attaining things, fun times, a drink here and there, and before I knew it, I was comfortable in the mud.

But now, oddly enough, sitting here in prison, I consider it *"pure joy, knowing that the testing of my faith produces patience"* (James 1:2-3). I firmly believe that faith that has not been tested cannot be trusted. I am convinced that I must stay active in this pen, and like the sheep, obediently listen to the Good Shepherd's voice, despite the pigs squealing around me.

There is no other way to actively wait while in this temporary confinement except to rely on the Lord to lead me, while prayerfully asking Him to use my story for His glory.

5. Gifts in the Storm

It's December and this month is always especially difficult for my family. My oldest brother, John, was taken from us on December 15, 2005. It was something we never expected, nor could have prepared for in a million years. Alivia, now six, was four months old when her Daddy went to Heaven.

I remember answering the phone that day as I walked back to my dorm at Temple University after taking a final exam. My mother's words, "Your brother John died," ripped me to the core of my gut. My eyes filled up with tears, but I didn't say anything; I continued walking to my dorm, quietly packed up, and drove home to my family.

From then on, I watched my parents navigate the foreign and treacherous pathways of grief. I watched them manage the practical while feeding the spiritual, and saw them consistently "look up" despite fluctuating emotions. I didn't realize it then, but I was learning how to handle heartbreak. I was learning how

5. GIFTS IN THE STORM

to get up even when you feel like staying down, and how to look for purpose when you are surrounded by devastation.

By every human standard, hope should have died that Christmas with my brother John. But because of our faith, we knew that hope was still very much alive. I witnessed firsthand God's gifts in the storm and watched Him carry our family through sorrow and set us on solid ground again.

On January 7, 2012, it will be two years since I've been here in prison and the words *"the other driver is deceased"* still haunt me daily. That same disgusting feeling in my gut and the tears that often follow are only a flashback away, every moment of every day. But I know now that in the midst of despair, and no matter how dark it is, hope is still alive. And there have been gifts in this storm, also.

One such gift, in particular, was a visit I received in prison. The warmth and compassion that I felt from this complete stranger in the visitor's hall confirmed that

> **In the midst of despair, and no matter how dark it is, hope is still alive.**

hope is, indeed, very much alive. George's beautiful daughter, Amber, had been killed by a drunk driver and he came to visit me—a convicted drunk driver—to thank me for what I've been doing and encourage me to keep telling my story. People like George and my parents remind me to keep looking up—and to keep looking for purpose—even when you are surrounded by devastation.

I get encouraging letters from people of all ages and walks of life, some from far-off places I can't even pronounce; these are my reminders to keep walking forward, just like my parents did that December day when the celebration of a birth was replaced with plans for a funeral.

If I could take it all back and bring Mr. Kap back to his family again, I would gladly give my life to do so. But because of my reckless choice, I am here in prison and an innocent man's family will celebrate the holidays without him.

So I pray for the Kap family every day, for healing and supernatural peace as they move forward without a grandfather, father, brother, uncle, and friend. I will continue to honor him in all that I do. *"O Lord, continue to give us gifts in the storm."*

6. Why Waste the Pain?

I have done several interviews since being incarcerated, including one for an A&E forensic documentary, *"Speed Kills,"* for the recently released series, *"Bloodwork,"* on the Crime and Investigation Channel.

Interviews are always emotionally trying as I am forced to face the hard questions and relive the events that placed me here. Not "hard" because I am in prison, but because I'm flooded with emotions each time I revisit that day, and the heartbreak I caused the Kap family. "Remorse" seems an inadequate term to describe how I feel about causing the death of an innocent man. Just the words, "causing the death" seem surreal as I write them.

One of the questions I am repeatedly asked: "What do you say to those who believe you shouldn't have a voice?" A fair question, and my response never wavers: "Of course everyone is entitled to an opinion, and I don't hold it against anyone for judging me. I judge myself the hardest. I didn't ask for a voice, but was given one."

If I were to sit in prison for the rest of my life, there would still be some who would choose to never forget, never forgive. I am the face of everything they loathe, a walking reminder of countless lives lost, and to "condemn the man" (me) seems a valid outlet for their pain and disdain. I understand that, but cannot understand allowing those feelings to interfere with a message that could potentially save lives.

> There is healing in knowing we aren't wasting our pain, but even more so, when we are using it for a greater purpose.

Should our failures silence us? If our fall can be used to lift someone up, then why neglect the chance to use it? Why waste the pain?

Right after my accident I was asked to speak at my local high school Bible Club and I can tell you it was the last thing I felt like doing. I wanted to crawl under my covers and disappear, especially in light of the community outrage toward me that was cropping up online and in the local paper. But I had always spoken out during the good times in my life, so it seemed only fair that I show my face in the midst of my shame. Anything less seemed like wasting the pain.

If I had acted on my feelings alone, I would have never shared my story that day at my local high school, or gone on to speak to so many students around the state prior to prison. In fact, my feelings would likely suggest that I skip the interviews, and blogs, and all of the uncomfortable and avoidable reminders of the devastation I caused on March 7, 2009.

But I cannot trust my feelings, or be governed by them—especially here in this chaotic and depressing environment. I choose to maintain a positive attitude, because my attitude is one thing I still control entirely.

A Corrections Officer supervising a recent interview, approached me and said, *"People definitely need to hear that message and you're doing a good thing here, keep it up."* He has no idea how those words encouraged me and motivated me to keep talking about my shame, even when my feelings advise against it. There is healing in knowing we aren't wasting our pain, but even more so, when we are using it for a greater purpose.

7. Seeking Approval

I spent most of my life trying to please everybody in general, and nobody in particular. It was the way I went about my day, but it was off. I was off. At the end of each day, no matter how well I performed athletically, academically, or otherwise, there was always someone I just could not please. It was impossible and I wore myself out trying.

But the opposite is now taking place, and from all places—prison. I receive mail from some I know and many I have never met. These letters flow in from all across the country: Florida, Texas, North Carolina, Oregon, New York and the list goes on... and continues on to include France, China, Africa, Germany, Saudi Arabia, Russia, and places I can't even spell. And the common theme among all is "approval," not for what I did to be in prison, but for what I am doing while I'm in prison.

I have finally given up entirely on trying to gain man's approval, and ironically, I am finally receiving it. And in prison, of all places. It's crazy to read "courageous" and "honorable" and my name in the same sentence after what I've done. *How does this even make sense?* I often think they may have made a mistake when looking me up online, and perhaps think I am the popular Christian singer, who also shares my name, Matt Maher. (I like his music and according to my mom, some arrive on our web page after searching for his concerts).

Regardless, I share the same opinion of myself as the Apostle Paul had, when he claimed to be, "the chief of all sinners," and sitting here in my "office" (prison bunk) staring at these letters of encouragement, I cannot help but see one word: *grace*. My mail does not match up with my wretchedness and heart of shame.

Life must go on for me behind these walls, and eventually beyond them, so each day I challenge myself to honor God in what I do and say. I no longer wait for man's affirmation or favor to determine how I see myself on any particular day, or let the good or bad opinions shape my worth. Instead, I focus on pleasing God in each area of my life, and trust that His light will overshadow the shame in my heart.

I take zero credit for who my mail says I am today, knowing that everything could change by tomorrow. So for now, I pray that I would never cause someone's faith in Him to falter because of my choices or actions, but that my life would lead others towards faith in Jesus Christ. But ultimately, I pray that I may be well pleasing in His eyes.

> **Only the grace of God can overshadow the shame in our hearts.**

8. The Rose of Confidence

A famous proverb states, "Pride comes before a fall." You can be certain that every fall leaves you on the ground with a decision to make from that downward position. If you need a picture on pride to teach a lesson, use my failure and the ripple effect of pain it caused.

My fall landed me in prison, but that is the least of the burden I carry and not the reason I share my "talk from prison." I share because I do not want to see anyone take a fall because they ignored their pride. The headline read, "Local professional soccer player involved in fatal DUI accident." That was the sickening obvious fact, but the underlying root story would never be read. My decision to drink and drive stemmed from a thorn disguised as a rose; the rose of confidence.

> **Pride makes you fake strong, but in reality, it keeps you weak.**

8. THE ROSE OF CONFIDENCE

Three years ago, this month, my pride was at an all time high. So high that I masked my emotional pain of a torn ACL in a professional soccer game at the Spectrum in Philadelphia. I knew my professional career was uncertain the very moment it happened; but the mental trauma only watered my pride further.

My pride wouldn't allow me to admit what I was feeling internally—fear for my future. Pride makes you fake strong, but in reality, it keeps you weak. And as I refused to admit that I was weak, I ignorantly chose to settle my pain in a bar full of sympathizers.

I had a choice after my first fall, my injury, but I neglected the proper response of reliance on my faith and God's bigger purposes. Five days later, I found myself wrapping my head around the State Troopers words, "The other driver is deceased." Those words are imprinted on my mind and heart and the mental pain fuels its purpose in my life.

> **He who believes to have removed all pride is never humble enough.**

Now in prison, my pride is at an all time low and that's a good thing. But I also know that he who believes to have removed all pride is never humble enough. The war I wage with pride is a daily battle. I now know that physically nobody wants to reveal the thorns in their character and that's why we display the rose.

But God knows best, and He allowed this mental thorn knowing it would keep my pride choked out. Prison doesn't humble the man, only man can humble himself. Pride is the original sin that took place in the Garden of Eden, and He still uses our falls to get our attention. I admit that my attention is undivided now and if an example must be drawn upon, please use my negative experience to do better.

My pride cost an innocent man his life. What will pride cost you?

9. Envision Your Future

After the accident and prior to sentencing day, I tried to envision my future. Friends continually asked me what it felt like knowing I was going to prison. I could never quite express the feeling in words. The analogy I used to satisfy their curiosity and my own impending reality was best illustrated from an amphibian's perspective. I would say, "Seeing and speaking of my future (prior to entering prison) is like a frog seeing and speaking of the ocean from a well." It could not be perceived.

Now currently in this "well of prison," and 27 months into my time, I realize that unlike the frog, my state of mind was already established to be content. Obviously, uncertain situations can make you feel uneasy or anxious, but I truthfully was not. I was not "fronting" or faking tough, but the only open logical position for me to lock my mind into was upward. So upward I looked and have not stopped since the moment the doors clanged and locked behind me.

Some would say logic is impossible in the throngs of uncertainties. But for me, it was my faith that made my logic sensible. I still cannot see the "ocean" from my perspective, but I choose to not look backward or forward—simply upward.

And now a new question has arisen: "What are you going to do when you get out of prison," which is just as complicated to answer as the pre-prison inquiries. Again, I will attempt to explain with the help of an insect metamorphosis—the caterpillar to a butterfly.

You see, I have my mind made up and as my eyes look up and out from this prison cocoon, the only logical answer to that question is to shed the past and fly. Without the intense struggle, the caterpillar couldn't transform into a butterfly because it is the struggle accompanied by perseverance that gives it the ability to thrive and, most importantly, to fly.

> **Whatever is contained inside a man will be revealed outwardly when being squeezed by pressure.**

Ultimately, the answer to these questions falls back to my mindset. I am fully convinced that it does not matter how deep this well feels or how confined this cocoon seems because as long as my mind is made up to be content—regardless of my circumstances—there should be no outward condition that controls my response.

Even envisioning tomorrow is still impossible—whether free or confined. But I can tell you what I do see. I see that whatever is contained inside a man will be revealed outwardly when being squeezed by pressure. And from my position now, the only view that matters is the One who is the Maker of all things.

10. Savoring Every Breath

Memorial Day Weekend is upon us again. From your position, that means summer is back at the Jersey Shore! The anticipation, the build-up, the planning—it's finally here. From my position, as a prisoner, this time can be very hard—knowing that family and friends on the outside are going to gather at parties, picnics, and barbecues for the summer's official kick-off while we are locked away from it all.

After Memorial Day Weekend, then what? Maybe the Fourth of July, a wedding, a vacation; but whatever is planned, all will come and go in due time. I remember the empty feeling that followed a much-anticipated event. It didn't last long because soon enough I was on to the next thing.

I do a lot of thinking in here, which guarantees serious reflection. So when holidays come upon me, I analyze where I was and what I was doing in times past. What I see is that what should have been *a time well served* from my position on the outside was actually spent planning on what I would do next. I

10. SAVORING EVERY BREATH

> **Staying in the moment, with mind stayed on God, fills you with joy and peace despite your circumstances.**

realize now that I was so preoccupied with the "next," that I missed the moment; missed time with family; even missed the blessing of freedom itself. Prison redefines the blessing of freedom.

Likewise, what could be *a time well served* to an inmate from this position is, instead, spent worrying about what his position is not able to do. While missing life on the outside, he misses out on the appreciation of the stillness—and he misses out on the time alone with God and the blessings of refinement through confinement.

"To worry" originally meant, "to strangle," and I see how worry strangles present enjoyment. I see futility in the way I used to hold my breath for what was coming next. By doing that, I missed the fresh air of the present. Even when you are done reading this writing, you will have forgotten most of the content and moved on to something else.

Memorial Day, originally known as "Decoration Day," is a time to honor those who have died in service to our nation. When I was on the outside, I didn't really think about that. Having had the experience of confinement, I hope I will never again miss the decorations of the here and now—right here, right now.

Regardless of my position (inside or outside), I will never allow anxiety for the next event or worry over potential events to strangle out the God-given time for me to "be still and know" (Psalm 46:10). I have learned that staying in the moment, with mind stayed on God, fills me with joy and peace despite my circumstances. Freed from the suffocating fears of anxiousness, I am—instead—thankful.

I am content in my position. Although that may not be freedom as you see it, neither am I holding my breath anymore. I don't need a weekend to kick off joy. I am savoring every breath.

11. To My Father

This *"Prison Talk"* comes with more appreciation and love than any amount of words could ever express. It is in this month of June that we are hallmarked into honoring our fathers, but this should never be limited to a single day. So I would like to honor the role of fatherhood while speaking directly to my own father, John Maher.

Dad, I love you and I am sorry all in one sentence. I know you do not want me to dwell on the past with yet another apology because you have already forgiven me unconditionally. So, Dad, I thank you for your love and the Christ-like example that you unfailingly model for all of your sons. Your unwavering integrity, without spot or blemish, precedes you, and your accountability to God goes without question. You have raised me up with such a solid foundation that though I have fallen

Pain is the fuel of passion.

hard, and now do my talk from prison, I have not crumbled; and though I shamed your name, you were only concerned with my well-being, while tenderly building me back up.

Presence is all that is required for stability. Your quiet strength shows through any situation—particularly under pressure, where the inward man's character is revealed outwardly. You set the standard of excellence for any young boy or man to follow.

Please know that although I am now classified a "convicted felon," the rest of my life will be lived so that this label will be part of my testimony of how amazing is our God. The shame and embarrassment that I brought to our family will not be left unanswered; likewise, the pain that I have caused so many people, especially the loved ones of Hort Kap, will not go unattended. You taught your sons to step up and take responsibility—no matter the cost.

Pain has fueled my passion, and I am finally clothed in humility. My only desire is to live for God, and to embody what you taught me: "Always do what is right no matter who is looking."

Happy Father's Day. Thank you for always being there in every way: in love, in concern, in correction, and in understanding. I am beyond blessed to call you my father, and I am beyond grateful for all you have done for me. I love you, Dad, today and every day.

12. What Have I Done?

There is clearly nothing that I can do to erase what I have done to be in prison today. I know this. I also know that no matter what I do from this point on, it will never be good enough in the eyes of some to rectify what I have done. I know this too.

I have actually been called a "hero" by some people for stepping up and owning my mistake. This makes me uncomfortable. It is hard to believe that there are many victims out there who have never received an apology by the person responsible for their reckless decision. I have also been called a "murderer." This makes me less uncomfortable for I am undeserving of the first term and have already called myself the second.

But for me personally, it is no longer about *'what I have done,'* for that is irreversible. Rather, it's about *'what have I done'* to warrant the first label. I will answer my own question and let you know that I have done nothing to deserve that label, for I am nothing. It has only been through God's grace that countless individuals have accredited my experience, and willingness to talk about it, with changing their perspective on life and possibly averting future tragedies.

I know some people would rather I shut up and walk to the gallows; but with that mindset, who becomes the murderer—responsible for more lives wrecked and ruined, more lives lost? It's not easy rehashing my story publicly, but I do so that others may do better.

> If we cannot take our messes and turn them into messages, how then do we teach the realities of life and the consequences of choices?

A hero I am not, nor am I a martyr. I deserve my sentence for what I have done. I made a fatal mistake. But if one cannot take his mistake and help others bypass it, how do we teach the realities of life, and choices, and failures, and redemption. How do we get up again?

I made a grievous error, I know this well, but prison has not made me pay for that error any more severely than my own heart. My own conscience. Prior to my sentencing day, I was asked by the South Jersey Traffic Safety Alliance if I would share my story through a program called, *"I'm That Guy."* In the span of three months, I visited 33 schools and spoke to more than 7000 students—putting my stupidity and recklessness on display, hanging myself every time—driven by the breath of hope to show young people how one wrong decision can flip many worlds upside down.

12. WHAT HAVE I DONE?

This did not bring back the deceased, Mr. Hort Kap, nor did it take away the pain felt by those who loved him. I know this. It may be, though, that it has prevented others from doing what I have done. This means there are individuals that will never have to repeat over and over in their head the dreaded words, *"What have I done?"* Perhaps you are one of these individuals. It also means there are individuals who have not had to suffer the unique anguish of being a victim. Perhaps you are one of those.

So, although I do not deserve to even have this *Prison Talk* with the reader for what I have done, I will continue to accept the invitation to share my words of faith to fill in the gap between being a hero and being a murderer.

13. August Tears

I've cried tears of shame publicly for what I've done and tears of regret privately for what cannot be undone. I've cried tears of grief publicly when my brother died and tears of joy privately for where he now resides. I've cried many tears of pain as a baby, as a teen, and as a man; but now as a prisoner, I cry a different kind of tear, one that expresses the words if my heart could speak.

These perplexing tears come not out of sadness or despair, but completely out of gladness and repair. They have had more meaning than any of my life's accomplishments because these are tears of humility and are the best cleansing my soul has ever experienced.

Such tears fall solely in recognition of God's grace, which I do not deserve, and have drained from my eyes uncontrollably because of who God is! It is not about an external freedom or a location, and it is not even related to my circumstances, because I am still locked up; but it's about an internal liberty

13. AUGUST TEARS

that is abounding, fulfilling, healing, and like a reflection in the mirror, revealing.

It is through these tears of humility that I see God's character and His amazing love toward me. This is not because I am godly, but because I am a sinner and God still loves me. In the Psalms, we see how valuable our tears are to God because He keeps an account of each one: *"You have seen me tossing and turning ... You have collected all my tears and preserved them ... You have recorded every one in your book"* (Psalm 56:8).

God's design for man is perfectly created in every aspect. His work is so marvelous and unique that He has placed His DNA in every one of our tears. If you look at a teardrop underneath a microscope, you will see that the saline crystals are shaped in the form of a cross. This cross symbolizes our "sorrow" and "mourning," but the Bible assures believers that our mourning will be turned into dancing and our sorrow into joy (Psalm 30:11) because of what Christ accomplished on the cross. He turned an instrument of death into an invitation to life.

Essentially, God wants to remind us that our tears

> **God's design for man is perfectly created in every aspect. His work is so marvelous and unique that He has placed His DNA in every one of our tears. If you look at a teardrop underneath a microscope, you will see that the saline crystals are shaped in the form of a cross.**

are important to Him. Jesus wept, and His tears proclaimed, "I know. I understand. I cry with you now, but you will rejoice with Me hereafter."

As if they are removing impurities from within, my tears rise to the surface of my eyes like dew on the grass—and I feel renewed, refreshed. From the contentment of my heart, my flowing tears disclose the truth of His promise: *"Weeping may endure for the night, but joy comes in the morning"* (Psalm 30:5).

14. Can You Hear Me Now?

Reflecting is a daily activity in prison—it comes with the territory. Not that it's forced upon you—it is solely activated by the inmate's forever wandering mind. As inmates mull over their thoughts, the results become apparent in their countenance. There are only two ways this can go—depression or progression. So here's the problem: Whether we are reflecting on an ugly past or reminiscing on the beautiful "thens," we are missing the "now." The past is a dead time zone, as God's voice is in the present tense; and He is saying, "Can you hear Me now?"

You don't have to be in isolation (or a prisoner in prison) to look back in time with regret. Ruminating on the past, and allowing the shame or the "what could have been" mentality

> God's time and calling are not held to a specific location, and that is why I am fully convinced that God honors whoever honors Him, esteems His time, and answers His calling.

wear on the face, shows others exactly what is preying on the mind: grief; guilt; despair; doubt.

However, it is precisely this dead zone site that has altered my sight toward good service. It has heightened my awareness that any activity must have productivity as its nature and an attitude that raises the bar consistently toward progression. Therefore, I often reflect about "then" to keep myself in proper check with right "now." Our calling to good service is only as active as our ability to hear God calling us to action with His ever-present words of "Can you *hear* Me now, My child?" God was calling me for a long time prior to my tragic downfall, but I missed the signs, the nudges, the messages. I let the noise of this world drown out His voice and set my eye on busyness and business, comfortability and complacency.

Now, in this time, I am beyond humbled to be on this "plan of calling" called confinement. It is not somewhere I would ever have seen myself, but it is the result of multiple ignored calls. I will forever be remorseful for why I am in prison, and I certainly deserve punishment and correction; I would be a fool if I didn't use this time for acknowledgment and reflection.

This lost time in the world's eyes does not have to be time lost in an inmate's mind. This daily activity of reflection should be a blessing for any prisoner because it is an opportunity to recognize our failures, faults, and flaws, and to change for the good; but most importantly, a time to 'Be Still' to hear God's calling.

It's sad, though, as many do not identify this time away as anything but an inconvenience. Instead of valuing this time as a humbling new beginning, they continue on in their old ways of dead-zone thinking—as if life has come to a dropped-call ending. Many neglect the opportunity to positively reflect to keep this reality in check.

God's time and calling are not held to a specific location, and that is why I am fully convinced that God honors whoever honors Him, esteems His time, and answers His calling. Hence, I cherish this time of correction. The battle is always won in the valley and lowlands, making good service for God available by simply picking up His call. My present response: "I can hear You now!"

15. My Position of Passion

"What could you possibly have to do that's so important at Mid-State?" One of the new inmates on my tier gave this scoffing, skeptical response to me when I said that I was not going outside for recreation because I had some important "stuff" to tend to this morning.

Because of the time crunch for this quick exchange, I had no answer that would make him effectively understand what "stuff" I consider sufficiently important so I had to leave him with a deficiency of information. Recreation in the yard and lifting weights are healthy pastimes, and each is beneficial in its own way; but the "stuff" I choose to do over rec and weights is more fulfilling. It is the time I spend looking into the mirror of God's Word, which I failed to do before prison. I now resolve to fully fill myself with "the right stuff."

However, before he exited through the open gate for the yard movement, I quickly assured him, "It's more important than what I was doing before Mid-State." I hoped this would remind

15. MY POSITION OF PASSION

him of the conversation we had the previous night, when he had asked me about playing professional soccer (before Mid-State) and if I was going to play again (after Mid-State). For me personally, the in-between time known as Mid-State Correctional Facility is more than a location, and I would consider it a "position." A position where I can choose to stay buried under my circumstances or one in which I can decide to rise above them, to be positive, to help others, to work on my writings, and to not allow a dark environment to influence my spirit. The position I choose is one that no man or system can take away from me, as my father repeatedly reminded me prior to sentencing day: "Matt, they can take your freedom, but they can't take your mind."

The tragedy that took place on March 7, 2009, initiated my position, which I will hold in my heart until the day that I die, but the in-between time for me at Mid-State has honed my position from pain to passion. No more old life of complacency—rather, a new life of consistency.

You see, in the several seconds after I discovered that there was a fatality in my accident of March 7, 2009, the violent blast of pain that blew through my soul was more than a public and shameful fall. This fall may have set my future of incarceration in stone, but it set something else in stone in my heart—and that was the position that I would honor my God, my family, and the life of my victim. What I now consider extremely important stuff to do at Mid-State is the daily habit and commitment of mastering this position by seeing my failures as the end of the old life and the beginning of the new life—to begin again, to rise again, and to do good where I can.

I focus on such thoughts because I know that whether I serve one day or 10 years at Mid-State, what I did to warrant prison will always be held over my head by some people after Mid-State. No one can tell me how far I've fallen when I have to recover from it day by day by day. It is a sober decision I make daily to get up and go on in mind, body, and spirit; and it has nothing to do with my location in prison. It is my choice; it is my position of passion. And it is one that God has used in my life to testify to His grace through disgrace.

> **Failure is not the end, but the opportunity to begin again, to rise again, to do good where you can.**

"But none of these things move me; nor do I count my life dear to myself, so that I may finish my race with joy, and the ministry which I received from the Lord Jesus, to testify to the gospel of the grace of God" (Acts 20:24).

16. A View Apart (How One Views the Time)

With curiosity, many people ask me: How is your time spent in prison? I would rearrange that inquiry and reply: "*Prison is spent on how one views the time.*" It is really simple when we are able to see things from the right perspective.

I cannot claim to always have the right view, but I am only able to respond to the original question about prison from what I call a "view apart": A view that relies on my faith and not my sight, and a view that is the opposite of the natural—it is, rather, supernatural; a view that allows me to feel "*Imprisoned by Peace*" (Book #1 of the *Core Conviction Series*, available on Amazon).

It is a common precept to say that all things will eventually pass, but what is done with the time that passes? Since I became an inmate of the State, my focus has been on utilizing the time in a deliberate, constructive manner.

My view apart is one in which my faith protects me from what I see around me, for there is nothing but chaos 24/7—crude words, lewd actions, aggression, racism, bullying, just to name a few. It is my faith that allows me to feel peace through this chaos. Having experienced forgiveness from my victim's family and my God, I try to view everything that assaults my senses with the heart and eyes of Christ.

Therefore, this view apart impacts how I spend my time, and for me it is the difference between ugliness and beauty. An inmate passes his time in ugliness when he chooses the wrong things to pass the time: complaining,

> **Time spent with a selfless heart will eventually show less of yourself and more of Christ in your heart.**

arguing, and dwelling with bitterness on the past. Likewise, an inmate passes his time in beauty when he chooses the right things: encouraging, learning, and pressing on in the present. When we spend time with either attribute—ugliness or beauty—we begin to take on its appearance.

In Ecclesiastes 3, it says, *"What profit has the worker from that in which he labors? I have seen the God-given task with which the sons of men are to be occupied. He has made everything beautiful in its time."*

I have given this phrase, "in its time," a lot of thought. Time spent wrapped up in ourselves will eventually come unraveled at the seams. Time spent numbing the pain will eventually increase the pain. Time spent filling our mind with toxic material will eventually spew out like vomit.

16. A VIEW APART (HOW ONE VIEWS THE TIME)

"In its time." Time spent with a selfless heart will eventually show less of yourself and more of Christ, who lives in your heart. Time spent using your pain as a passion will eventually help others with their pain in passing. Time spent filling our minds with God's word will eventually flow forth like rivers of life.

"In its time." Our appearance shows out what we allow in. I spend a lot of time working on the ugly in my character by using the beauty of Jesus to polish me out. I see triumph in my tragedy because I know God makes beauty from ashes. I see freedom in this time. I see character sharpening in this time. I see peace through confinement in this time. God's will be done, in His time!

The way we inmates spend our time will eventually make or break our future upon release. What emerges from the cocoon of a common caterpillar when given the proper time? A beautiful butterfly. "He has made everything beautiful *in its time*."

Even with the ugliness that surrounds me—the cursing, the lust, the evil, the fights, the hate, the envy—I am committed to spend this time in beauty with a view apart; a view that sees outwardly what I have committed inwardly: self-control, goodness, contentedness, love. Only by God's grace in this time, will this time come to pass.

17. God Sees the Heart

January 7th will mark three years to the day that I woke up in my own bed, but went to sleep that night in a prison cell. I began the day in a suit, but ended the day in a jumpsuit. January 7th was sentencing day for me. The figures of 5-to-10 years tossed around by the lawyers mattered less to me than the sentences I would speak to the family of my victim, Hort Kap. Those 5-to-10 minutes were foremost in my mind. Those words of remorse were the plea bargain of my heart.

My father drove me to court that day. It would be my last taste of freedom; and by the day's conclusion, I would get my first taste of confinement. In hindsight, neither left a bad taste in my mouth, but the emotions I experienced between arrival and departure from the courtroom were too gracious to ever be properly savored.

I was instructed by my attorney to be aware of my facial expressions and demeanor at all times, as the media would be there and would try to obtain the worst picture of me—the perpetrator—for their primetime sound bites. However, I felt that only a cold, heartless man would be able to maintain stoic composure under such conditions. If I could have, I would have left my heart for Hort Kap's family to dispose of as they wished—but God had other plans for it.

So much was said that day on my behalf by friends and family, and much was said against me by the prosecutor. I learned some amazing insights about the life of Hort Kap from one of his daughters; I sat immobile and at attention as I listened to the gut-wrenching story of how one son found out his dad had been killed. I deserved the shame I felt, and that sickening emotion is just as real to me today.

> The love of God is so radical that it never leaves a heart in the same condition it finds it in. He takes us from grace to grace. He sets at liberty those who are captive. He see's our heart, not our face-sheet.

I hope the Kap family knows that I will always greatly esteem their loved one's name and life. I know that sounds trite, but it is the truth straight from my heart. I left the courtroom that day on a mission to right my wrong in any way humanly possible.

I went to bed that first night in peace due solely to the forgiveness extended to me by the Kap family. I slept in a frigid 6-by-8 cell at the county jail—without a bed, blanket or pillow. I lay shivering on a thin mattress, left vacant on the concrete floor. Yet, I was warmed from within. I reflect back and wonder how many others had gone before me in the same dismal cell and felt closed in and bitter for it? By God's grace, I knew I was exactly where I needed to be—broken, and open, and better off for it. I was unchained.

I was awakened very early the next morning for transfer to the State Central Receiving Facility. It was freezing outside, and snow was falling once again. Shackled and handcuffed, I was placed in the back of the transfer car. As we pulled away, the officer in the passenger seat turned and opened the sliding glass. He said, "You'll be all right. A lot of us can be in your shoes. I know you want to see the paper." And he handed it through for me to see the photograph on the front page—a picture of Hort Kap's son extending to me a hug of forgiveness. I immediately recalled my initial instruction to "watch my demeanor," and I smiled at the revelation that God's lens always sees the heart.

My life is not my own anymore. This mission of redemption with God is possible because He sent His own Son to be born and to offer His perfect life for sinners like me. And the love of God is so radical that it never leaves a heart in the same condition it finds it in. He takes us from grace to grace. He sets at liberty those who are captive. He see's our heart, not our face-sheet.

18. The Birth of New Life

I'm pretty certain that most people have already packed up the last remnants of their Christmas decorations—after all, we are now into the New Year. But this is prison, and since I didn't have any lights to take down or ornaments to put away, the demagnification of the holiday season doesn't exist—and frankly, that reality alone puts things into a deeper perspective.

Often in our culture, the spirit of Christmas gets packed away with all our yuletide emotions of "peace and good will." Instead of delighting in Christmas by carrying the birth of Christ into the New Year, we succumb to the de-lighting of our joy and the quenching of our lights; and we carry the birth of New Year's resolutions right into the death of those same short-lived commitments, temporary passions, and holiday props.

Three years ago, my Christmas celebration heralded my impending incarceration—a prison sentence that officially began on Jan. 7. But something happened in my dingy prison cell on that seventh day of January 2010, that only the Christmas story can explain. You see, God had already closed off all doors for comfortable housing options prior to Mary and Joseph's arrival in the little town of Bethlehem. Such closed doors led them to a stable, where animals were lodged. Here, in these unsanitary and foul-smelling quarters, Jesus was born. Lacking a crib or cradle, His parents placed Him in a feeding trough; a manger was His bed.

> **Sometimes God will close a door to open a heart.**

This dismal location was predetermined by God to bring His Son into the world for not only the eternal salvation of man, but to instantly set man free. Of all the places in the world for a King and Savior to be born—a dirty, stinking barn inhabited by livestock. Remarkable! Why would God choose to place His Son in such lowly circumstances? In order for God to become flesh and partner with mankind to see His will worked out through us.

In my desolate, dreary cell on Jan. 7, 2010, the Christmas story came alive to me for the first time in my entire life. I mean *really* alive. I had left Christmas behind in December, but a closed cell door brought me to my own type of stable. It was right there in that dank, secluded prison cell that I re-birthed and re-committed my life to my Lord and Savior Jesus Christ. Like peace and joy that only the beholder can explain, my manger instantly had light. I knew I was facing over 2,000 days in this dark environment, but I had been set free—and no prison cell was going to put out my light.

18. THE BIRTH OF NEW LIFE

Over 1,100 days later, with three Christmas seasons in prison, I have learned that to partner with Jesus is to use my incarceration as an incubator—and not because of anything that I can do for myself, but because Jesus walks with me, one day at a time. The growth in this incubated time will only be demonstrated in time. Even Jesus, the newborn babe celebrated at Christmastime, had to grow before He could speak out.

"And the Child grew and became strong in spirit, filled with wisdom; and the grace of God was upon Him" (Luke 2:40).

I consider myself nothing more than a lowly servant, but I'm a Christ-carrier and in Him I have my liberty. Without the birth of new life, I would remain confined in an unlivable stable—unstable.

I may be confined for a reckless reason, but the Christmas story for me is no longer confined to a time or season. Happy is he who brings Christ into every aspect of the New Year.

19. Scars Tell a Story

I have an ugly scar, but I have made the commitment not to hide it because of Jesus' example. He bears His scars—even to the point of honoring the apostle Thomas' disbelieving response in His resurrection from the dead by exposing His gaping wounds as proof of Who He is. The obvious difference here is that my own sin caused my scar *and* Jesus' scars; but I am thankful that God has graciously allowed me to use my scar to show others what I have done, and where I have been, and hopefully to lead others to do better.

You see, every scar has a story to tell. In order for the wound to heal, the original scab should not be picked at. Like this prison experience, the scab is the protective healing agent that covers this wound. The scabbing must be allowed to have

> Because of God's grace, we don't have to hide our scars. Because of His grace, His scars are in fact covering ours. By His stripes we are healed.

19. SCARS TELL A STORY

its way without interference so that the wound beneath may resolve itself, well below the surface, in order for the flesh to be built back up properly for useful service.

Eventually a scab falls off, and leaves behind the scar. The scar serves as a testimonial of past pain, present healing, and future purpose. Our scars—every single one of them: big or small, deep or topical—have a monumental reason in our lives. At the very least, they teach us that healing is possible. Like Doubting Thomas, people will see our scars and believe that delivery from their wounds, their pain, and their shame is possible.

I've humbly committed to exposing my own weeping wound day by day of this journey because healing is by God's grace alone. I firmly believe this opportunity of writing exists because I have allowed this repulsive scab called prison to form the necessary protection that enables my wound to heal—mentally, physically, and, most importantly, spiritually. There have been days when I wanted to pick at this scab—when I wanted to do away with it—but this would not be of any use. Many may see my scar as nothing but an eyesore, but God sees it as a time to teach me to wait—then soar. The prophet Isaiah writes: *"But those who wait on the Lord shall renew their strength; they shall mount up with wings like eagles"* (Isaiah 40:31).

If only blood and puss were the substances to drip forth from my wound, then my scar should never be exposed. Unless the scar is dripping with a message of renewal, it should remain hidden in shame; and the prerequisite for the message is to highlight the mess caused, while at the same time promoting the wound that is healed.

Society is entitled to be mad at me and condemn me, and I've joined the people in that campaign. I'm MADD too. I oppose drunk driving—who better to expose the grotesque results of such actions than one who caused the wound, endured the scab, and is committed to sharing the message of the scar? I shoulder my responsibility; and like the example of my Savior and Healer, I will expose my scar to help other people know that we can survive a fall, we can be forgiven, we can get up again, and ultimately we can lead others to faith.

20. The Man in the Mirror

I'm going to get straight to the point, man. I could not look you in the eyes four years ago today—nobody could. Not that I did not want to at the time, but it would have been hard to see the soul when the head was bowed so low in despair. The eyes reveal the soul. Then again, I did not need to see you directly to feel your shame, your rejection, and your grief. Any attempt at words exchanged would have fallen on deaf ears. I did not want to hear you, nor you me. But we must agree now! *Can two walk together, unless they are in agreement?* (Amos 3:3)

If I had verbalized my thoughts on this day four years ago, you would have buried yourself deeper in sorrow—even to the point of no return. So I held back, not just for your sake, but for our sake. I kept back my thoughts because I desired to walk in agreement with you then, as I do now, but if I told you certain things you would not have been able to see outside the box that "confined." You were "closed in" at the time, but I have spent much time studying your eyes over the past four years. I never looked into them as intently as I do now. Much has changed indeed.

Today, I see into your eyes clearly; and I want to remind you of some important motivators as we move forward together in agreement. Never forget that you are more than the choices you have made. If someone tells you differently, tell them you are more than the sum of your past mistakes. You may have done what they said you've done, but you do not have to be who they say you are. You are new. Besides, it does not matter what anyone else sees in you for only God knows the heart.

I will tell you what I see, though, that I may encourage you to never give up. I no longer see shame, but salvation. I no longer see rejection, but redemption. And I no longer see grief, rather gratitude.

You are content because your heart has been cleansed, and this affects your vision. Now that we can finally see eye-to-eye, it is crucial that our agreement includes never again looking down on one another. Others look down. You now look up!

On this day, you have a fresh spark about you. A different glow. A shine. This was not so four short years ago. In fact, it was the complete opposite: Your heart was wrenched with pain. Your heart still feels the pain daily, but you must continue to move on and begin a new thing. I want to tell you that I am proud of you and thank you for letting me see

> **You may have done what they said you've done, but you do not have to be who they say you are.**

sin personified; for without your remorseful pain, there would be no passion fueled again.

God needs us both, and I'm going to need you to watch my back when I walk away. That is all I can ask of you, and I'm not talking to anyone else but you! Especially on a day like today.

I'm talking to the man in the mirror …

(*In honor of Hort Kap, 3-7-09. Forgive me.*)

21. Cloud 9

I have been "down" for 39 months. "Down" is jail lingo for "incarcerated." Yet, I have remained "up" in mind, body, and spirit. "Up" is my term for "content." I am thankful for not having faltered in my daily desire to remain up and positive in spite of the dark circumstances that surround me. This has nothing to do with me, but rather Jesus Christ in me. You may think prison has made me "too spiritual," but prison has afforded me a front-row seat to experience the power of a God who truly does give light in the dark. It is a fact that I cannot deny, neither will I hide it.

I reside in a "crooked" place, yet my vision remains straight. I am consistently upbeat not because of visits, mail, meals, television or a release date. Yes, these can all serve as uppers in a down time, but my state of mind should never be swayed by outside factors or favors.

When someone exhibits extreme highs and lows so vividly, they are labeled "bipolar." Like the North and South poles, the mindsets of many inmates are divided to such dire extremes. But the bipolar behavior generally displayed in here is not the exhibition of the brain disorder, but is symptomatic of an imbalance of the mind. I call it "circumstantial instability," and this observation comes from my field of study in my 24/7 environment of chaos.

So this is what I see. Inmates may walk around depressed all day long because of mail call and the circumstance of either getting a negative message or no message at all or because of a missed visit on the weekend. They are like zombies and refuse any human interaction. If one tries to break through their stupor with emotional encouragement, that caring individual is aggressively rebuked.

Then, one will observe the mood of these same inmates suddenly altered by something as minor and inconsequential as a chicken patty for lunch. Instantaneously, they are jovial and even playful in their words and actions. It is like the "Cloud 9" effect.

"Cloud 9" is a state of perfect happiness or bliss. Interestingly, "clouds" symbolize the manifestation of heavenly activity; and the number 9 means "an end which brings a new beginning." (Spiritual trivia: Jesus died at the ninth hour.) When the inmates' material appetites are met in a happy way, they are placed in the euphoric circumstance of being on Cloud 9.

And that is the problem with being "circumstantially unstable." The simple remedy is not medication, but meditation and mental dedication. The meaning of "meditation" depicts

> **Chewing on God's Word gives you sustenance and stability through any depressing and trying time.**

what a cow does as she grazes. She chews the cud over and over again, extracting every nutrient. Likewise, meditation is how we ponder and extract every truth we digest or consume—and this process most assuredly provides the ultimate *Cloud 9* consistency.

That is why I am always "up." Chewing on God's Word has given me sustenance and stability through a depressing and trying time. I am not bipolar in my circumstances because I have committed to Jesus' way and will; and I walk with Him as my equator, my equilibrium, my balance.

If I relied on the circumstances around me, I would be depressed—and you would be depressed reading about it. So I tell you what I feel inside regardless of what my eyes are receiving on the outside. I feel inside exactly what I have committed to in my heart: stability; balance; consistency. *"For God has not given us a spirit of fear, but of power and of love and of a sound mind"* (2 Timothy 1:7).

It is now 10:45 A.M. as I write this piece, and 25 out of 38 men are sleeping. The only thing that will rouse all of them from their semi-conscious state will be 11:30 mess call. This is what I see every day. This would be depressing if my mind allowed it to be. I could lay "down" with my environment or stay "up" in Christ. It is not a hard choice.

22. The Telling of a Tear

You can't see them coming down from my eyes, so I have to make this essay cry. In honor of my mom's tears that have left a trail from what her eyes have seen, flowing down to where her heart has leaned. A faith blossomed by weeping waters, for all of us to follow her stream of example through our very own desert experiences.

Please allow my tears to write out my heart as each drop on the paper tells of a different smear; but as Jesus has wiped each one away from drop to drop, these smears have been the mark that clears and eventually heals. She has cried her fair share, but none more telling than the ones that have been squeezed out of her by her sons.

> **Don't question your tears. Rather, go on a quest with your tears and they will lead you to a God who is always near.** *"You keep track of all my sorrows. You have collected all my tears in Your bottle. You have recorded each one in Your book"* **(Psalm 56:8).**

This mother of mine can't tell me anything that her Christ-like actions did not already express. If she said it to me and my brothers, that's because she lived it as a God-fearing mother. She birthed four boys into this world, and God gave her the perfectly untimed blessing of seeing her oldest son (John) off to heaven. That's not a failure for a godly mom as the faithless would see it. Purely, that is the testing of faith as God knew my mother would see it.

God was not surprised by our family's tragic outcomes—He knew that through the hard-pressing on every side, this mother of mine would allow the pressing to push her harder in Him. Her tears still come with the thought of John's passing, but you should see the path that they have paved directly to his daughter, Alivia. Tears that say to her, *"Daddy's with Jesus now, and they both are watching over you from above."* And a few more for those looking on, *"Don't cry for me—cry for those who have never experienced God's love."*

You can't see them coming down from my eyes, so I have to make this essay cry. In honor of my mom's tears that have washed away any doubt about suffering successfully by faith, even when one of her son's actions was a reckless disgrace. With three sons left in this world, God gave her the perfectly untimed blessing of watching her youngest son (me) go off to prison.

That's not a failure for a godly mom as the faithless would see it. Purely, that's knowing God works all things for the good of those who love Him, and that's how God desires us to see it. God was not shocked by what I had done—He knew that through the hardSHIP I was responsible for setting sail, this mother of mine would sail directly toward Him.

Tears still come with the thought of what I have done and where I am, but you should see the waters that have been stilled because of these weathered tears. Tears that say to me, *"My son, you must follow Jesus now, and be sure to do all things for the Kingdom's gain."* And a few more fall for those looking on, *"Don't cry for me—help me wipe the tears of those drowning in pain."*

My godly mother's example watered my family's faith through her tears, producing rivers in the desert and clear sight through all the smeared plights. "*Mom, you can't see them coming down from my eyes, so please allow me to make this essay cry. You've seen my tears of the past, but by your example I've learned to release them to oil my soul for the present. Let us remember that our tears are capable of writing out what God's Word declares to those who grieve: that He will 'give them beauty for ashes, the oil of joy for mourning, the garment of praise for the spirit of heaviness, that they may be called trees of righteousness, the planting of the Lord, that He may be glorified'*" (Isaiah 61:3).

23. Faces Frozen in Time

There are so many facets to a person's life, yet it is common to fall into the trap of remembering a person because of one negative face. One label. "Isn't that 'so and so,' the one who got divorced?" "Wasn't he addicted to drugs?" "She's a felon." "Oh, him—he dropped out of school." "She got pregnant in high school."

Labels—all of which conveniently categorize a person's entire life, veiling his or her character behind one negative face frozen in time. One noticeable hardship. One bad season. One awful decision.

I presently write these thoughts with my "face sheet" lying right next to my word processor. A prisoner's face sheet is his resume: his one-dimensional biography acted out by him and

> **I am who I am by the grace of God, and I am a new creation in Christ. I live by the label He has placed on my life. His record.**

published by somebody else—often at the expense of another. On this piece of paper, one's classification is reduced to a charge and a status. According to my sheet, I am no more than a felon. A prisoner of the state. An inmate number: 314525E. Charge: Aggravated manslaughter. First degree. My criminal record.

But there are many more degrees that make up the person of Matthew Maher and even far more faces that I have worn prior to the mug on my face sheet. For some, their face sheet may be accurate and a fair summary based on their recidivism rate. But for others, it is a surface evaluation of an isolated circumstance—a tragic one for sure, but nonetheless not a total picture of one's history. However, this face sheet label becomes the label synonymous with a prisoner's face; it follows him wherever life leads from that point on.

Through my journey, I have met a few whose one moment of faulty judgment will define them forever. A family man with a promising career gets into a fight in a bar, and the other party is injured. The husband, father, and rising star winds up with a new label: felon. And a face sheet that erases 20 years of an illustrious resume. The end result will always be a life evaluated "with prejudice."

I understand how my face may recall in other people's minds the egregious act that I caused. But I must admit that I sometimes ponder with mind-blowing regret how one reckless decision erased all the other facets of my life. Twenty-four years of being a "normal" kid, who also managed to earn a few labels such as: a high-school honors student; a full-scholarship recipient; a double-major graduate of Temple University's Fox School of Business. Twenty-one years as a student-athlete, who managed to earn accolades and awards, championships and records. Eventually earning other labels—first round draft pick and professional.

All these labels were just surface facts to the multiple facets of my life prior to March 7, 2009. Yet, in spite of my past labels and present label, I proudly wear a new label—a label that takes every facet of my life, the *beauty* of it and the *beast* part of it, and gives me a new record. A new face. A new label. *New*.

There are those who will always remember me for what I've done, and I'm OK with that. They will label me "felon" and "murderer." I can handle it because I know who I am and Whose I am. I am who I am by the grace of God, and I am a new creation in Christ. I live by the label He has placed on my life. His record.

However, for the sake of others, I urge you to think before you attempt to fit another person's entire life into one negative description.

"Therefore, if anyone is in Christ, he is a new creation; old things have passed away; behold, all things have become new" (II Corinthians 5:17).

24. Light From Darkness

I attempt to transmit light from a dark prison, for even a single match can illuminate an entire room. Yet, I often think how most media sources report from the "light of liberty," but their message is almost always inherently dark for such is the nature of news! However, from the dark backdrop of prison, "*Prison Talk*" may be able to talk someone out of a prison of pain or problems.

I don't have all the answers nor do I claim to be something I'm not, but I know light and dark when I see them. And when these contrasting elements are constantly visible as they are in the house where I live, then the particular element can be easily detected—and respected accordingly. Whether you reside in a dark prison, carry a dark past or wrestle with dark problems, God allows such darkness so that the light of His will can be seen more clearly than the world's messages. It is God who commanded light to shine out of darkness (II Corinthians 4:6).

A jeweler knows this concept well. To attract our eyes and inspire admiration for his diamonds, he displays them on a black backdrop. Thus, whether it is a velvety black drape or a dark past, consider it joy that God's light wants to show you off as the diamond that you are. (That sure comforts me!)

I'm in prison and under steady, unrelenting pressure. But to a man with faith and conviction, this place of pressure becomes a cave with purpose. It is in the darkest caverns of the earth, in an environment of immense pressure and very hot temperatures, that carbon deposits are transformed in a natural refining process into brilliant diamonds.

> Whether you reside in a dark prison of sorts, carry a dark past or wrestle with dark problems, God allows such darkness so that the brightness of His glory in you can be seen more clearly against the black backdrop around you.

It may seem ironic that the jeweler then resorts back to the darkest cloth in order to display the valuable diamonds most effectively. Likewise, it is against the darkest messages of the world that God displays the beauty of His diamonds most effectively.

In prison, there are many potential diamonds-in-the-rough: many unpolished, extremely hard individuals who may have much to offer society. But they are left untouched, or perhaps further damaged, by their environment. Rather than cleansed or purified, such inmates are crushed by the pressure of prison.

However, this truth is not only held to the place of prison: It can be a free man's mountain of problems that render him useless. The pressure of his problems, too, may crush him. Or he may be like a diamond buried in an unmined cave, because it is both the exacting use of pressure and the appropriate extraction from the dark confining cave that allows the light to shine.

Trials, tribulations, and temptations—when these dark difficulties come (and they will come), take them to God and allow Him to do what He has done from the very beginning: pull light from darkness.

25. Well Traveled

I often wonder what it's like for my parents when they come to visit me. I frankly don't know; nor can they fully comprehend what prison life is like for me. I can tell them and assure them that all is going well. But I'm their son, the youngest of their four children; leaving me here in prison can never be normal. It can never be comforting.

I often wonder what they talk about on the way here. What do they feel upon entering the prison yard and viewing the barbed-wire fencing and tall watchtower manned by an armed guard? Pulling into the prison parking lot is far from pulling into a stadium or an apartment complex.

"We're going to visit our son this weekend," would be a typical statement from my parents throughout the years as they regularly visited Anthony at Mercyhurst College in Erie, Pa., Mike at the United States Naval Academy in Annapolis, Md., and yours truly in Philadelphia at Temple University. They often traveled far distances to watch Anthony play during his

25. WELL TRAVELED

professional soccer career, and they had just begun doing the same for me. My parents are well traveled.

Those must have been much-anticipated trips, with many proud moments; and upon the visit's completion, they left us where we were supposed to be—where we worked to be. They left us free as we all know freedom. Free to pick up the phone. Free to check in at any given time with a call or a text. Free to follow them home if we so chose.

But not these weekend trips to prison. The same way they came, they must certainly go. Upon entering this place, they must stand patiently in a single-file line as they wait to walk through the metal detector. They are required to leave all personal items in their car, and then they are inspected through a routine frisking and pat down. They leave the visiting hall when commanded. And that departure time varies week to week, depending on the number of prisoners that need to be body-checked and cleared after a visit's end. All of these infringements must be a constant reminder that they are in a different world—not of their choosing.

"Visitation terminated," shouts a corrections officer. All the visitors must move to the front of the hall, while the inmates must line up against the back wall. Young children immediately begin crying and cleaving to their imprisoned father. It must appear chaotic and unnatural in their minds. Fathers don't leave their children.

It's time to go. No questions asked. No more small talk. No additional time allotted. My parents must leave their son—their youngest child, who once had such a bright future. It can't be like leaving a college campus or a sporting competition. It can't be.

> **The future is always bright with hope when your faith is right in Christ.**

I don't know what it's like for them. And they don't know what it's like for me. But I can tell you this: My future is still bright with hope because my faith is right in Christ. My parents may feel sick in their stomachs when they have to leave me here, but they are leaving me in a freedom that would never have existed had I not been here.

I attempt to consider my parents' journey as they come and go on these weekend visits, that I may cause no more pain. Yes, my parents are certainly well traveled—and on a path that they never could have envisioned. But God knew. God knows our every step and even our every stop.

26. The Reality of Faith

"The future cannot be ill, when your faith is well." From where I am writing, those are not empty words. Have you ever thought about what faith means to you? In the Bible, *"faith is the substance of things hoped for, the evidence of things not seen"* (Hebrews 11:1). But this is not so much a definition of faith; rather, it is a description of what faith does. Faith is not wishful thinking. Faith is believing and perceiving into existence what you have not yet seen.

Consider how easily you place your trust in an elevator. When you press Floor 7, you know that platform is going to lift and release you at Floor 7. Seems too logical, you say—but that is exactly what faith is: treating "things hoped for" as reality accomplished. "I need to make it to the seventh floor," you say, so you press 7 and off you go. That's faith! The expectation that the elevator will hold you, while you trust it to do so. That's reality!

Another example of faith is when you travel across a bridge. You know the bridge is going to support you as you

> **Wait at God's promise until He meets you there, for He always returns by the path of His promises.**

cross in midair from one side of solid ground to the other. You can't always see the source of support, but you still do not hesitate to proceed with that reality. Driving with faith is trusting in the "evidence of things not seen." Likewise, using an elevator or a bridge is no different than trusting God to lift us when we "push His button" or carry us when we "drive over His promises." Our faith activates His services.

Faith does not solve every one of life's problems, but it will bring you peace through your elevator lows and your bridge highs. From day to day, the future is unreliable; not one of us can make plans or predict with absolute certainty the course of events. I know this firsthand. I am continually asked, "What are you going to do when you get out of prison?" My response: "Not sure, but I know I will be following God's direction through open and closed doors." It is my faith that assures me God holds my future, and it is in that hope that I will not be disappointed.

Without hope and a vision, the future will become ill. I remember back when I was a child, life seemed so simple. I was playing in a Little League game, and the other team was beating us: 11 to nothing. During an umpire's time-out, I walked over to the fence to pick up a stray ball when an older gentleman asked me what the score was. I replied, "It's 11-zero, Mister!" He said, "Wow, you guys might as well give up at this point." I quickly objected with childlike faith, "Give up? Sir, it's only 11-zero, and we haven't been up to bat yet!"

> **The future cannot be ill, when your faith is well.**

Hope keeps you from giving up no matter what the world says about your circumstances. Many may see defeat, but what they tend to forget is: They haven't given themselves a chance to bat yet. I like to encourage the guys in here by telling them: If they can see it, they can be it; and by faith, they should walk in it.

We may be in this dugout called prison, and you may be in the freedom of the field. Both alike are watching other players continuously score, but hope knows that we have not been up to bat yet; and faith is capable of overcoming any deficit or turning around any defeat.

The fact that I write a column from prison is the very "evidence of things not seen," and the very "substance of things hoped for." I may still be down by the world's standards and by the scoreboard, but I'm stepping into the batter's box. I'm pushing 7 in the elevator. And I'm crossing that bridge.

27. How Well You Show

It's not how much you know, but how well you show what you know. So what do I know, and what qualifies me to tell you what I know? Well, I know well what I know; and coming from prison may not qualify me to tell you what I know, but it certainly should intrigue you to consider what I know. I know peace from a chaotic place. I know joy in misery's company. I know liberty, though confined.

How many people know so much in principle, yet show so little in action? So for me personally, how can I know more and then give less? I'm committed to give what I know by living what I know. Example always trumps precept. Some may call that babel; I call it Bible!

Throughout my growing-up years, my mother often repeated this admonition: "Matthew, you may be the only Bible somebody reads today." She knew more and just wanted me to be more. I cared less and that is why I gave less than my best. But what I know now isn't because I know it all—it's because I

> **Example always trumps precept.**

know well what it is my mom told me after all. I am the only Bible that many of my peers will ever read; and that's not knowing it all, that's giving my all to let others know.

How well do I know what I know? Well enough to show and tell without saying a word. It's not easier said than done from this incarcerated position. The more done and less said becomes easier when acted out from a liberated position. And the only way to do more is to know more to show more. Knowing is showing.

It may be a challenge to get my peers to read their Bibles, but I can make it easier for them by challenging them to read *me*. My mother was right with what she told me long ago. She knew that if I lived to show what I know, then others would care how much I knew because my knowing would show them how much I cared.

I have learned that our example is the essence of how well we know what we know. Consider my words for now for what they say about what I know or wait until my release to see how I show what I know. Like my mother told me: I may be the only Bible somebody reads, and I am committed to being a good read.

28. Polarized Degrees

I graduated from the Fox School of Business at Temple University with a BS in Business Administration, and a concentration in Legal Studies. In other words, I got myself a worthy business degree, but this esteemed education did not prevent me from getting myself another type of degree—first degree aggravated manslaughter. So, what went wrong here? Well, first of all, just because everything seems right, we cannot assume that nothing is wrong.

I astutely recognize that even though I attended four years of college and passed every class with honors, I missed the educational value that such time should have accomplished within me. You see, attending classes, passing courses, and even obtaining a degree does not always equal retention. I may have earned myself a degree, but in retrospect I realize I did not *learn* myself the degree. I was there, but I wasn't all there, and I took that time for granted. Before I knew it, my four years were done, and graduation meant that I was a professional scholar and eligible bachelor. The scholar turned to a pro soccer career, and I applied the advantages of bachelorhood to my social life. Ultimately, my degree meant nothing to me because the time spent under that degree was not used effectively or efficiently.

> To be effective is to do the right thing. And to be efficient is to do things right.

Much has changed since receiving my BS degree; and though that one took four years to complete, I earned another degree in a single night. However, this degree was conferred before the "education" began. The education is better known as *incarceration*. Now I possess two different degrees, and the felonious one has been the more relevant—not because of what I did to be under that degree, but because of what has been accomplished *within me* during the time under that degree.

So, what went right here? Well, for one, I have not allowed this detention to deter me from retention. And further, though I recklessly earned this "first degree," I've learned to effectively and efficiently use the time under this degree. To be effective is to do the right thing. And to be efficient is to do things right. And lastly, similar to my prestigious college degree, this felonious degree does not define me nor refine me. It's just a piece of paper that is used at this point in time to confine me.

So, what happened here? Well, I now have two degrees with polarized outcomes. And I realize that the "educational values" therein are only retained and gained according to how I chose to use these different times under the different degrees.

My education at Temple University: $100,000+. Turning my prison incarceration into a temple education: priceless.

29. Alivia's Eye's of Hope

Before my formal sentencing date sent me to prison, I was stuck between a rock—my impending incarceration, which was set in stone—and a hard place, still being free in my community. It was no man's land for me—knowing that with each passing day, I was one day closer to the uncertainty of certainty. I had no idea what to expect, but I knew there was much to anticipate.

Regardless of whether there was any truth in this, I felt the overwhelming weight of the terrible impasse; I was chained like a slave to it. The pervading feeling that held me captive was the belief that all eyes were on me everywhere I went. I felt glances and gazes, all weighted with looks of disgraces. True or not, whether this was the view or not, I felt it. Eyes that locked me up before I was locked up.

During this time before prison, I was afforded quality time with my family, not having anywhere to go or anything to do … but wait. And during that time, I experienced the liberating expression of another set of eyes. No matter where I went with my niece Alivia (then 3), those blue eyes staring at me from the rear-view mirror set me free. They blinked to the resetting of blue with eyelashes that waved grace upon me—a reminder of life from loss. *Her life,* which began just four short months before the loss of her father. Those eyes spoke to me without her little life ever comprehending the impact she was having upon me, her disgraced Uncle Matt.

It was not unusual for my mom to ask me to pick up Alivia or drop her off—brief excursions that gave me the opportunity to secure her in her child-safety seat, turn on some children's Christian music, and ask her to sing to me. She would. In her squeaky voice, she would set me completely at ease from the condemning eyes that I believed awaited me everywhere I went. Behind Alivia's blue eyes was the "stair" of heaven. Her eyes took me up one step at a time. And that peaceable feeling I had then before prison, I have now while in prison. I'm reminded of one biblical meaning behind the color blue, which is symbolic of heaven.

God knew I needed her heavenly blue and accepting eyes back then, staring at me through the mirror, reflecting liberty into my soul. And now locked up, I look into the mirror of the Word, and heaven's eyes grant me serenity all the more. I realize now that it doesn't matter how other people may view me or even how

> **And now locked up, I look into the mirror of the Word, and heaven's eyes grant me serenity all the more.**

I sometimes view myself, because as long as "blue eyes" behold me, no condemnation will ever again hold me. I was a slave to those feelings when I was between the rock of prison and the hard place of my community. No man's land on my way to a land where I'd be a no-man.

I'm 48 months here now. I'm still a no-man. But Alivia's eyes remind me that beyond this blink of a life is where heaven lies.

30. A Few Years Ago

I was unexpectedly taken back, way back, when a Corrections Officer (CO) said to one of my peers in front of me, "I told Matthew that a few years ago."

I thought, *"A few years ago!"* Wow! Weird! Those words sounded surreal, and I was jolted by the realization of how much time has passed since my arrival in prison. Forty-nine months in the same barricaded building, like a fortress; the same dingy and cheerless interior, like an abandoned basement; the same intense and chaotic environment.

The CO's statement brought me back to the very beginning of my prison bid and all that has happened along the way from then to now. I started to think of this length of time, "a few years ago," in relation to: minutes, days, weeks, months—adding up to years.

> **It's not about the day's duration;
> it's about a person's donation to the day.**

30. A FEW YEARS AGO

What is contained in a single year? Twelve months. Fifty-two weeks. Three-hundred sixty-five days. Eight-thousand, seven-hundred sixty hours. Five-hundred twenty-five thousand, six-hundred minutes. Now quantify that to my "few years."

While some things about prison do not change, other things in here can transpire and change radically in just one second. Hence, "a few years" in a place like prison expresses much more than a quantity of time. The measurements cannot be accurately calculated nor condensed to simply "years" without comprehending the demands required of an individual to complete just one day in prison—that is, 24 hours, 1,440 minutes, 86,400 seconds. Add to that the countless ticking of the mind's thoughts and the many decisions that must be resolved by that mind in limitless encounters. The result is an equation of an unstable population, held in limbo, sealed in a vacuum, with too many variables.

Some may be waiting to explode—the threat of violence is a constant presence. Others cannot handle the time and are defeated within Day One of their imprisonment. A one-second decision to give up affects years of prison living. Despite surrendering—imploding before the specter of prison—these individuals soon perceive that the war is long and extensive and consists of daily battles because time isn't measured in the length of the day, but in the strength of how well one fights the day.

It's not about the day's duration; it's about a person's donation to the day. Tens of millions of seconds come down to a choice of two options: victim or victor. All I know is that God's grace has continually poured out on me in abounding proportion to the load and unforeseen weight of time. "A few years ago," I did not see the value of this time, but today my attitude of victory sees "a few years ago" as battles faced and won each moment of each day—the measurement of time weighed in character development as I handled such ordeals one second by one minute by one hour.

"A few years ago" rests on my shoulders as a donation to my character development—not duration of time chronologically developed. So while time pushes down relentlessly, I've learned to push up victoriously; and the hands of time are not what moves me to victory—rather, the hands of Christ that were stretched from 9 to 3 on the cross accomplished this for me.

Hindsight is better than foresight. We can all look back "a few years ago" and see what God has brought us through. One second. One minute. One hour. One day. One week. One year at a time.

31. Tragedy Warrants a Response

The greater transgression than the tragedy itself is a failure to respond to the tragedy itself. The right response is the key that unlocks the success in suffering; the wrong response, however, is the noose that tightens the grip of suffering.

Suffering occurs at different levels, as do the responses. But one thing is certain: Real faith makes all the difference. Whatever the reason tragedy has struck, it still requires a response. Suffering will have its way: It will open you up or close you in.

> **The right response to tragedy is to shoulder it, not hang from it.**

Remember, your insight of tragedy doesn't have to be dictated by other people's eyesight of the tragedy. Consider me, for example. I was the cause of tragedy, but that doesn't exempt me from having to choose the right or wrong response of heart. Some eyes that view my disastrous event will only ever see me in a noose. That refusal to see an individual beyond his tragic circumstances prompts me to wonder: Who is the one really hung up?

My responsibility to tragedy is to shoulder it, not hang from it. Failure to respond in the right manner keeps the sensation of pain on the nerve, when what is required is that the suffering produces new insights and vision to navigate the pain on the nerve. Not to numb it, but to learn from it.

There is no public poll that determines a response, nor should there be. Rather, it is one's personal role that delivers the right response. You see, when success is unlocked in suffering, it produces a soul that someone else will need to feel in order to get through their own tragedy—like a message of encouragement written in Braille on your soul, the soul of a fellow sufferer. In that vulnerable moment, their need for insightful comfort far outweighs their eyesight of the reason behind your tragedy.

Tragedy is universal and inescapable; many are not sure which way to go in their pain. They may have a key in their right hand and a noose in the other, and that is why your heart can help lead them to right response. The right helping hand brings success and not suffocation. The right helping hand is always part of God's plan. The right helping hand is the insightful hand that extends God's heart through suffering.

"Blessed be the God and Father of our Lord Jesus Christ, the Father of mercies and God of all comfort, who comforts us in all our tribulation, that we may be able to comfort those who are in any trouble, with the comfort with which we ourselves are comforted by God" (II Corinthians 1:3-4).

32. What Matters Most

Life on the inside of prison—oh, how dirty it is! An inmate can diligently clean up his area day in and day out, but the dust and grime persist—and flourish, like mushrooms after a soaking rain. This is the "house" I live in, and literally the "grounds" I keep.

I try my very best to have a neat, presentable area. Actually, it doesn't hurt to have my OCD (obsessive-compulsive disorder) tendencies kick in, inherited from mi mama, and I am left with no choice but to rigorously maintain my "house" in perfect order—from my properly made bed to my carefully aligned sneakers beneath the bed. A neat presentation of my personal items is the closest I can get to feeling like I am able to attain any routine standard of cleanliness in this place.

No matter how tidy things look on the surface, however, if an inmate does not scour the unseen parts of his area daily, then the exterior appearance is nothing but a façade. Underneath the lockers and hidden from view are the pervasive grunge and debris. Close examination would expose another type of filth that matches the staleness of prison air, the dismal bleakness of the institution, and the impenetrable clutter—but is far worse because it inhabits the being.

Many of my peers make sure their hair, beard, and skincare needs are pampered each day, only to "jail" within the jail. ("Jail" is an activity done during a prison day.) The same people, with their same faces, deem showing off the outer features more important than devoting the same amount of attention to cleaning and grooming the inner character. So perversity, pornography, foul language, and aggression inhabit the outer environment. In reality, that filth is grown beneath the surface of a man; like a deadly mold, it eventually sneaks up and contaminates the atmosphere.

It's no different from life on the outside, where we spend so much time and energy making ourselves look presentable—washing and polishing our surface areas, but not being mindful that it's below the skin's surface that matters most! I'm not against the upkeep of the exterior, as is evident from my space, but I'm speaking figuratively about keeping up with the cleanliness of our inner selves.

You can paint and repaint a rusty statue to make it appear new, but the paint will chip away and reveal the true deterioration. I have learned that if the rooms in my "house" are not swept clean, then a mown lawn will fail to impress for it is the inside that reflects my true self.

32. WHAT MATTERS MOST

Jesus said, "Woe to you, [...], hypocrites! For you cleanse the outside of the cup and dish, but inside they are full of extortion and self-indulgence. [F]irst cleanse the inside of the cup and dish, that the outside of them may be clean also" (Matthew 23:25-26). The inner man matters most!

33. I Wonder

I wonder what it will be like to taste what I've tasted before, but not the way I'll taste it now? I wonder what it will be like to feel what I've felt my entire life but haven't felt since my incarcerated life? I wonder what my eyes will soon see, though they've seen the sites long ago that I now long to see? I wonder how I will be with those I've been with before, those who think they know me, but truly know me no more? I wonder how I will respond to new relations, new situations, new complications, when I've known them in the here and now, but I haven't experienced them outside of here to even know how?

I can only imagine...

I wonder what clanging keys will make me do in freedom, when I know they pose no threat to me like here in prison? I wonder if I'll avoid opening a door, when I've done so plenty times before, but in here never, lest they think you're leaving by force? I wonder how controlling a light switch will change my sleep; and then there's the question of how will I respond when

I lay down and there isn't a peep? Will the silence create noise in my mind, the way the noise around me now creates a peaceable time?

I can only imagine...

I wonder if I will struggle with human relations, when in here you are nothing but an object of authoritative degradation? I wonder if carpet under my feet will make me feel incomplete, knowing that cement has been my sole's retreat? Will a leather chair make me uncomfortable compared to my plastic throne? Will a computer with a screen be helpful and kind to me or is my word processor an extension of me that I cannot leave behind? I wonder what life will be like after prison, and I'm afraid that I'll be institutionalized forever in this condition?

I can only imagine... because none of the above is a problem to a man who self-examines. How could I worry about life after prison when I have not been conditioned to be prison-like even while in prison? And further, I'm not an animal that has trouble adapting, like a wolf trained to be a dog. A wolf's a wolf! You can put a bird in a cage, preventing it from flying but that doesn't mean it will forget how to fly when let loose. You see, a conformer takes on the behavior of his situation, but a transformer changes every situation because of his behavior.

> **A conformer takes on the behavior of his situation, but a transformer changes every situation because of his behavior.**

I wonder not what many wonder on behalf of me. Instead, I wonder what God will do, the more I recognize His many wonders on behalf of me.

34. Nowhere to Go but Up

There's nowhere to go but up from here. I'm not saying it's going to be easy; but I'll tell you this, it's going to be easier from here. I've been through too much to even flinch at anything the future has to offer. *"Yet not I, but the grace of God which was with me"* (I Cor. 15:10).

I've felt the suffocating grip of loneliness. Yet when it was done squeezing me, Jesus was still with me. I've felt the nauseating feeling of helplessness. Yet when there was no more help to hold onto, that's when I discovered that God's hope was holding onto me. I know what it's like to taste despair and swallow shame. Yet both ingredients have been part of the necessary batter that brought to the surface a purpose and a passion, which would never have been released *otherwise*. And that's just it, only the wisdom of God could have filtered so much good out of a pit.

It's usually in the ditches of life where you feel the lowest and dirtiest; but at the same time, it's your fallen position that gives you every reason to start climbing. Up and out, to truly know what being clean is all about. *"But by the grace of God I am what I am"* (I Cor. 15:10). And I am coming out stronger than I went in.

You see, claiming to be strong is not wrong when you know it's not your strength. *"I can do all things through Christ who strengthens me"* (Phil. 4:13). So I will rely on His strength supply. Not like Superman—"up, up, and away"—but with the Son of Man, Who takes me up in the Way; for *He is the way, the truth, and the life* (John 14:6). Christ is the only Way that completely dissolves the presence of strife.

> **Claiming to be strong is not wrong when you know it's not your strength: "I can do all things through Christ who strengthens me" (Phil. 4:13).**

There's still more glory to be had for God. And this place of prison was nothing more than a launching pad to Him. What about my crime and punishment, many may wonder. The cross of Christ already redeemed it—now that's the only wonder! *"You are the God who does wonders; You have declared Your strength among the peoples"* (Psalms 77:14).

There's nowhere to go but up from here. *"And His grace toward me was not in vain"* (1 Corinthians 15:10).

35. My Final Talk From Prison

"The way to peace and victory is to accept every circumstance and every trial as being straight from the hand of our loving Father."—Mrs. Charles Cowman

I place pen to paper to herald my final talk with you from behind the walls of prison. And I give honor where honor is due. First and foremost, to my Lord and Savior Jesus Christ, for without Him I can do nothing.

Much appreciation is owed to Art Hall for contacting my mother, Andrea Maher, with the proposal that I write this column. Thank you for taking the risk that I had something worthy to say. I am grateful for the professionalism of the *Herald* staff and for the hometown hospitality.

I would also like to recognize Cherri Olsen for her accurate eye in editing my flamboyant thoughts. Her mastery of the English language and the proper application of Associated Press style always took my writing to another level.

To my mother, who acted as mediator between the newspaper and me; and who faithfully typed my handwritten columns, provided me with feedback, and met all the deadlines in her typically well-organized fashion: Thank you, Mom.

To the readers of the *Cape May County Herald*: I humbly thank you, for without your hearts and eyes these words would never come alive. This voice would never have been evidence that faith, hope, and love make it possible to survive.

Where from here? I'm about to walk out of these doors on my second release date Aug. 3, 2014. You see, my first release took place on Jan. 7, 2010, and that was the liberation most relevant to my well-being. I discussed that gracious release in an earlier column titled *"Set Free by a Hug"*. Forgiveness was given to me by my victim's son, Noun Ung, and it came in the form of a hug.

Since that sentencing day, about four years and seven months ago, I've been on a purpose-driven trajectory to glorify God in my circumstances and to honor the life and memory of Hort Kap in spite of my circumstances.

I have learned this much: If Hort Kap's family has forgiven me and even endorses me, then it does not matter what other people may think of me. You cannot silence a voice from the grave of failure sent back to speak life. Many may believe that I don't deserve a voice, and I agree with them; but truth be told, I don't have a voice—the Voice has me.

Every platform comes with a sphere of influence and a corresponding degree of accountability. So I ask of you one thing: Please, don't stop "reading" me, because there is more for you to see from me. And if you do see me, don't ask how I'm doing since leaving prison—instead, let the sight of me remind you of the grace of God, and then tell me how you're doing because of God's grace in your life.

> You cannot silence a voice from the grave of failure sent back to speak life.

I will be exiting prison and re-entering society in one week. It doesn't feel like I've been gone that long. To some, it may not have been long enough, and to others it was too long; but to my Father in heaven, it was the divinely appointed time that developed a man out of a boy. Not a day early, nor a second late.

It's time for me to go home. It's time for my spiritual liberty in Christ to meet the physical freedom of life. It's time to put action behind this diction. It's time to make my living the manifestation of my writing.

This is my final *Prison Talk*. From here on out, I'll herald the message: #iCONVICTION.

36. Holiday Musing

Dear Santa,

I am writing this letter from prison. I hope my location doesn't hinder my chances of reaching you, even though for the past three Christmas seasons you have not made any attempt to visit nor leave me any presents. Is it because I am deemed a naughty person? I have other visitors that come and spend time with me, and they always bring *"good tidings of great joy"* (Luke 2:10). One such messenger, Pastor Victor Hudson, enters this prison weekly to minister to us "bad people" because he knows that if he serves us, he is serving in the spirit of Christmas all year long (Matthew 25:40).

Santa, you should hear the gospel preached through Pastor Vic. He is a true saint, who reminds us that we too can be saints when we are spiritually set free. Can you imagine that? Even we prisoners can be set free! Which reminds me, why do they call you Saint Nick? I just recently learned that the word "saint" means "set apart." Santa, are you set apart? Well, surely

36. HOLIDAY MUSING

you must be since so many people worship you as the spirit of Christmas.

I know you've probably made your list and even checked it twice, but because of my current label, "felon," I doubt I've made it over to the nice column. How do I get off that naughty list of yours? Pastor Vic reminds us each week that God nailed His list to the cross and willfully died once for every person on your list, whether naughty or nice. In fact, God now only sees those who accept His Son as nice, or righteous, because by the blood of Jesus, He paid our price.

Santa, this means that those who are on God's list, or in His will, will have peace and eternal life, all for God's glory. And get this: All I had to do was just believe to receive because of the Baby that was conceived.

So being on His Christmas list is all that truly matters! So many of us here in prison were excited to receive that gift.

Santa, don't take my letter the wrong way; I'm just trying to wrap my mind around the reason for this season. It seems as if the Yuletide has changed. I mean, I have seen how important it is for families to try and get a picture of you with their kiddies. Yet, watching small children from afar, I have sometimes witnessed holiday cheer turned to holiday fear at the thought of sitting on the lap of a stranger garbed in a red velvet suit.

Conversely, I've read in the Bible how parents would bring their children to Jesus that He might put His hands on them and pray. Those children didn't cry, Santa, and I bet it was because of what they saw in His eyes. Compassion flowing and mercy showing, not just a candy cane and a ho-ho-ho'ing.

And speaking of candy canes, did you know they are chock-full of symbolism? For Christians, the hardness of the candy represents the solid rock of faith. The shape of the candy is that of a shepherd's staff, representing Jesus as our Good Shepherd, and if you turn it upside down, it forms the letter "J" for Jesus. The white represents the virgin birth and the sinlessness of Christ; the red stripes symbolize the wounds Jesus suffered on our behalf—*"by His stripes, we are healed"* (I Peter 2:24). The peppermint flavor reminds us of hyssop, a minty herb used for cleansing and purifying in biblical times. Because of its association with purification, hyssop branches were used to brush the blood of the Passover lamb onto the doors of the Israelites; and when the Lamb of God hung on the cross, a hyssop branch was used to lift him a drink of vinegar.

In closing, I'm not sure if you'll get this letter, but since you can "see me when I'm sleeping, you know when I'm awake, and you know if I've been bad or good"—wait a second! That jingle sounds like a description of God.

I hope you're not trying to replace Him, Santa.

Sincerely.

36. HOLIDAY MUSING

*These transitional thoughts were written only a few
days before Matthew's release on August 3, 2014.
They were posted on his website and Facebook.*

3 days left. "Wow" is all I can say because it feels as if this all just began yesterday. And that's been my attitude of gratitude since day one of this long run, where answering the following question has motivated me to keep my eyes fixed upon the Son: *What do you do when you've found yourself in between yesterday's tragedy and tomorrow's triumph?*

Well, first of all, you don't worry about the time, knowing that God is always working even while we're waiting. Time can seriously get in the way, because there's no such thing as a deadline when you're operating out of eternal time. The goal is to be still — yet still moving, trusting that God will move when it is absolutely best for you.

Next, you cannot dwell on the past, for what's done is done; and what you do today will surely affect your tomorrow before it has even begun. Yesterday's tragedy and tomorrow's triumph are certainly interrelated, but it's only in the present where faith can be regulated and your life can be liberated.

Finally, but not entirely, you shouldn't ever look too far down the road. I'm not saying don't cast your vision, but I am saying don't let your idea of the vision to cast you. It may not look like what you envisioned, and if things start to go in a different direction, then your vision must be flexible enough to take on a new perception. For yesterday's tragedy to turn into tomorrow's triumph, it is mandatory to have today's trust. And that's exactly how I can say "wow!" I've trusted the Lord with all my heart and diligently desired that He would trust me.

In the "time of in-between" that most would call prison, God's economy has made me use this in-between time as training. And that's what I recommend you do if you ever find yourself in between yesterday's tragedy and tomorrow's triumph. Live in today's trust!

INTERLUDE—POST PRISON

Matthew's column in the Herald Newspaper would undergo a name change. Originally known as Prison Talk, it would be re-branded as #iCONVICTION, but today it is presently known as Truth Over Trend. You can view these columns by visiting here:

https://www.capemaycountyherald.com/opinion/columns

37. The #iCONVICTION Movement

I've been on the field, pro; I've been behind the wall, con. Now I'm back from the grave of failure with iCONVICTION. What is #iCONVICTION? I like to describe it by what Bible teacher Howard Hendricks once said, "A belief is something you will argue about. A conviction is something you will die for!"

It seems many people are getting their individual identities from the world around and outside them—the iECONOMY (iPhone, iPad, iMac, iMessage, i-EVERYTHING). This is fickle and fleeting—as opposed to a core conviction within a person, which is valuable and affirming. Since the message we are putting out is usually determined by the conviction we hold within, then perhaps it's time to get back to an internal and *eternal* core conviction—where our personal resolve is governed by God, regardless of the world's pressures that surround us.

> **Pressure produces passion as a friend, but this same pressure can produce fear as a foe.**

There will always be pressure, and it's either a friend or a foe depending on how we let it mold us. I feel this pressure as of late, not because I am under it but because it is under me. It moves me forward and motivates me to PRESS on for SURE. Against the odds. Against the sways of the world. And even against the ways of my own will.

While I would prefer not to be vocal or visible, God's grace cannot be contained nor can it be kept hidden. So the pressure pushes my iCONVICTION out, like a volcano that was dormant for years and is now ready to burst forth. That best explains this transition from prison to freedom. Despite my desire to stay under the radar for the sake of comfortability, I cannot due to the way this pressure pushes me to accountability. It's not my beliefs that garner respect from others; it's my conviction that instigates reflection for others.

At times it is overwhelming because speaking out promotes acceptance or provokes rejection—the people hate me or they love me. Both responses to "my story" produce pressure, and I must balance both ends of the spectrum in order to remain whole and usable by God.

Almost immediately following my release from prison, I was given a variety of speaking opportunities: I was interviewed on national radio; I sat on a panel at the N.J. Wardens Association for Re-Entry Initiatives; I spoke at a community college, which launched a series of speaking engagements to high-school and college-aged youth, funded by State Farm Insurance. I wholeheartedly stepped up to these platforms, knowing they are offered by God's grace alone. And they created connections with very different audiences.

Yet, in every situation I encounter, there is still pressure. But here is the key: The more I own my conviction, the more value I bring to any situation. The greater pressure that is within me is the only pressure I want to govern me. *"He who is in [me] is greater than he who is in the world"* (I John 4:4).

Pressure produces passion as a friend, but this same pressure can produce fear as a foe. I have to make a choice on a daily basis. Fear may be ever present, but courage pushes through the fear and makes passion the driving force.

So here we go. Join the #iCONVICTION movement, and together we'll begin to learn how to own it.

38. Out of Perspective Pain

I rub the scar on my knee, the residue left behind after surgery to repair a torn ACL (anterior cruciate ligament) and meniscus, and I am reminded that the tragedy I caused began by misunderstanding pain. Like a serpentine river and its many branches, the scar formed of multiple incisions runs down the center of my kneecap. Six years later, these still-numb lacerations are reminders that *pain out of perspective* is *pain without purpose.*

After I discovered I had injured my knee in the last professional soccer game I would ever play (though I did not know that at the time), I allowed out-of-perspective pain to leave me without proper perspective. At the time of the injury, I thought, "Woe is me," which automatically had my future in professional soccer hanging in the balance. I had already weighed my future against the pain and believed I'd never play again. I was right—but not because of my knee injury, but because my out-of-perspective pain led to infinitely greater pain caused by me.

38. OUT OF PERSPECTIVE PAIN

I thought I knew pain on March 1, 2009, the day I tore my knee. I would have said I was well acquainted with pain, that I was familiar with pain, that I understood pain. But just six days later, the early morning of March 7, I would learn about real pain.

March 6 fell on a Friday (as it did again this year), and I was feeling sorry for myself about my possible career-ending injury. So I hit the Philly bar scene with friends. Drinking away my pain. Hours later, I would feel real pain with the realization that I had ended someone's life. This pain, which is with me as vividly today as it was at that moment, has taught me about my out-of-balance perspective and the arrogant me.

> **Pain out of perspective is pain without purpose.**

I had missed the major lesson in the minor pain. You see, the initial pain should have humbled me, and I should have limped straight to God with all my pain—physical and emotional.

It didn't have to come to this. Humility can be learned without tragedy. I challenge others to humble themselves before out-of-perspective pain does it for them. Learn from my negative and make it your positive. That's the challenge within #iCONVICTION.

I once again rub the scar on my knee, and I am reminded of all that God has healed in my past. This scar has a story to tell about the purpose of pain and sorrow. Scars may be ugly, but God sees a story.

39. Formative Years || Formative Prayers

They say that your formative years are the crucial years for personality development; I believe that. But I also believe there is something even more crucial to your personality development, and that's the "formative prayers" that lead to your spiritual development. Such formative prayers are said without you ever knowing they were offered up over your head. They rise to heaven from an unconditional heart, while you are still learning the terrain of the earth. And even when the world seems to grow you with age, it is the power of those prayers that ultimately shower you with grace.

With that foundation in mind, I believe my spiritual alignment and character development have been protected—not only because of disciplined child-rearing, but also due to the fervent praying which came from the heart of my beloved mother. She has prayed for my life to be used for God's glory. This wasn't a responsive prayer to my tragedy; this was actually a progressive prayer from my youth. She prayed in this diligent manner

39. FORMATIVE YEARS || FORMATIVE PRAYERS

over all of her children—for our futures, our families, and our spiritual usefulness. She prayed for her sons to be men of character, conviction, and community. Her prayers went up, and I see clearly now how the answers have come down.

> Be assured that delays are not denials. In fact, the greater the delay, the greater the glory that will be displayed.

I know I am being used of God, even through such adverse circumstances; and though this may not have been the answer my mother expected from her prayers, it was the answer God allowed. It was the outcome of failure that would bring the greatest glory to God; and because God always knows better, that is all I need to know to be better; and that's all I need to know to ultimately surrender to the answered prayers of my mother for me to do better.

I owe much to the faithful prayers of my mother, and I owe all to the constant faithfulness of my God. He has not forgotten a single word she has prayed on behalf of her children, and that is a word for every mother out there who has travailed in prayer on behalf of her children.

Mothers, be assured that delays are not denials. In fact, the greater the delay, the greater the glory that will be displayed. We, sons and daughters, praise you for your loyal and unfaltering love on our behalf.

40. The Essence of a Father

Lately I have been rereading my mom's book, *SLAMMED: Overcoming Tragedy in the Wave of Grief*, and the experience has led to grief-filled tears mingled with grateful memories. Traveling backward in time is impossible, except by thought alone. For people of faith, those periods of reflection can be a comfort as we see how our past events—the good and the bad—were all part of God's purpose and plan. For my parents, that even meant the loss of a son.

Something about that event struck me hard as I read the written account in Mom's book. Something I've always known, but never deeply considered or pondered. I still can't fathom it, but the words recorded on the page vise-gripped my heart and moved me to such emotional anguish that I can't imagine what the actual effort did within my own father's heart (*SLAMMED*, Andrea Maher, 31):

> […] His firstborn son had died, his namesake, and there was nothing he could do to change it.

40. THE ESSENCE OF A FATHER

John took on the onerous tasks related to preparing a body for burial. He identified Little John's body at the morgue. He picked out John's clothes and even dressed him for the viewing. He made all the funeral arrangements—and found himself alone as he stared at a death certificate that had his own name staring back at him. [...]

And I thought how strong and loving a man must be, how loyal and kind: In quiet solitude, to be able to cleanse and care for his son's lifeless body while publicly presenting a steady composure for his other sons to see.

My thoughts began to harass and torment me as I grieved to think of what I had put my father through, after he had already walked through such a tragedy with my brother. Yet, most striking—and most comforting—is what I am left with through it all: that my father's love never wavered; in fact, he loved me all the more and taught me to be more.

Christ-like character is the essence of my father, and that is why he is my earthly role model. He may appear stoic because he manages his emotions like a poet—with metrical flow of his heart's beat, controlling what he

> For people of faith, those periods of reflection can be a comfort as we see how our past events—the good and the bad—were all part of God's purpose and plan.

rhythmically shows on his sleeve. Great sensitivity interlocked with strength in humility.

So I find myself thinking about my father, and how he has walked uprightly through the death of his oldest son and the incarceration of his youngest son. I dragged his name through the mud, but he never stopped treading along with me to the other side.

I'm truly thankful to be blessed because of my father's walk. *"The righteous man walks in his integrity; His children are blessed after him"* (Proverbs 20:7).

41. Set Backs Can Be Set Ups

It was around this time last year that I anxiously awaited my release from state prison. After serving four-and-a-half years, I had no idea what to expect beyond the walls that I had come to know so well. Countless inmates had told me to never get used to the dismal setting on the inside; but I realized early on that, like a diamond, I must accept the setting the jeweler chooses for me.

I write figuratively in using a diamond and its setting to explain my motivation for accepting my imprisonment as the catalyst for my future freedom. The setting that "holds" you can very well be the setting that eventually displays you. A diamond with the right setting is a diamond that makes an impression.

Last July was actually one of the hardest times, even though it was the closest month to my release, and all because of a prison break that put my entire unit on lockdown. It was the day before the Fourth of July, and a fellow inmate decided to take Independence Day to a whole new level. As a consequence

> God specializes in recycling good from evil and creating beauty from ashes.

of his fateful decision to declare physical freedom for himself, we were all subjected to 24-hour shakedowns and degrading strip-searches. In fact, I was strip-searched more times in that final month than in the entire four-and-a-half years.

It was a very uneasy time due to everyone's emotions and frustrations, which were running high. Prisoners and officials alike were caught up in the unstable tension. To be locked up is one type of animal, but to be on *lockdown* while locked up is an entirely different beast.

I bring up this time in my life to encourage the individual who thinks his circumstances are hopeless, and the one who believes that no good can come from such bad; to uplift the person who imagines she is so close to the resolution, yet feels so far away. Consider my life and story to see how every setting and every setback can in fact be the setup that God desires to use for His glory. I cannot erase my past, but forgiveness has erased my guilt and shame. God specializes in recycling good from evil and creating beauty from ashes. I accepted my setting early on, and I still appreciate it even today.

The shakedowns and strip-downs that I experienced in this month last year right before my release were nothing more than the necessary tests to make sure the diamond did not come loose. Using another appropriate analogy, the final pressurized month was simply the last phase of metamorphosis. After many days encapsulated in the tiny shell of the chrysalis, a butterfly is ready to emerge.

God will use every bit of space in your situation to refine you and define Him. He proves His love through our pain. He grants us purpose through our problems. He will reveal Himself through the person who allows Him to do so.

42. A Place of Projection

Everybody has a platform, but not everyone knows it. A platform is a place of projection—that's actually my definition. When you think about *where* you stand, then you can think about *what* you stand for and *how* you project that stance. You see, your place of projection is any place where your life takes on a reflection. Thus, your platform is everywhere you go and everything you do. It projects and reflects what is important to you: your priorities; your plans; your purpose.

You may not look at your vocation or even your recreation as a platform, but that's because you may not realize how every situation can be used as an opportunity for impact. Whether it's of the mundane or something birthed from pain, the platform under you is the plan God has given you.

So the question remains, "How are you using your platform?"

I often think about my platform and the messages that are projected on a daily basis. From social media to how I conduct

42. A PLACE OF PROJECTION

myself in social settings, and from public performance to behavior done in private. If we desire to have friends or followers, than we ought to take seriously the responsibility to be a friend and a leader. Both positions involve projection.

So the question remains, "How are you using your platform?"

I once was a pro soccer player. I, not too long ago, was also once a prisoner. Now, however, I am an author and instigator and a Student Ministry Team leader. Yet every single place I have been or will be is a platform that God has chosen for me, that I may be an influencer for Him.

No matter your career choice, you can still choose to turn your career into your calling and be God's agent in that workplace. There are people around you who need to see what the reflection of hope looks like through your countenance.

> **Whether it's of the mundane or something birthed from pain, the platform under you is the plan God has given you.**

There are co-workers watching you who need to see what the projection of faith does when the going gets tough. Every place you stand and show face is a place where you can be the connection to help others understand grace (unearned favor by God). That is the very point of every platform—to be the ambassadors of God's kingdom on earth.

So the question remains, "How are you using your God-given platform?"

43. This Present Comfort

I am sitting on my comfortable couch with a 55-inch flat screen in front of me. I just controlled the lighting to my liking and before I go any further—please excuse me—I'm going to grab a quick drink and snack from the fridge.

Okay, I'm back now, still comfortable, but at a loss for words to type. And I'm humbly reminded how this is the complete opposite of how I used to write while in prison. There—I never had an ounce of trouble writing a full page of deep thoughts graciously surrounded by peace in the midst of so much chaos and so little comfort.

Back then, I typed on an antiquated Word Processor, positioned on an empty box on my bed. The box, (often pulled from the trash), was used to elevate the machine to keep me from slouching while typing. My bed served as my desktop, and there was nowhere to place my knees, as my plastic green chair would be tucked up against the metal frame of my bed. And instead of

43. THIS PRESENT COMFORT

having a wall or TV in front of me, the view ahead was beds and bodies coupled with constant commotion and verbal pollution.

Yet oddly—there—I was never at a loss for words and actually wrote a blog a day for almost five years as well as my monthly *Prison Talk* column. Now—out here—I struggle to write just 2 blogs a week, even as I sit in comfort.

People ask me all the time if I have nightmares about my time in prison. I don't correct them, though I'd like to say—"You mean my time in freedom?" You see sadly, you never really know peace until you feel chaos. You never come to see the beauty of liberty until it's experienced through the ugliness of confinement. And it was—there—in prison—where I knew true comfort because of true discomfort.

I readjust myself on this couch and realize how comfort is actually a spiritual disservice. I'm at a loss for words because in this comfort it seems as if my words are getting lost. I mean, they are inside of me, but they are so contrary to my comfortable setting. All of my needs are being met by me. Such a controlled environment: I control the lighting ….I control the temperature… I control the TV…I control what I'm going to eat and when….

These are my struggling thoughts, because they are not finding their peace through any struggle. Yep! I miss being so pressed in the midst of confusion because this present comfort seems like nothing more than a spiritual distraction.

> **You never come to see the beauty of liberty until it's experienced through the ugliness of confinement.**

44. The Triumph of Trouble

Trouble is never a welcomed guest in a home, and when this unwanted visitor barges its way through the door, the surroundings become uncomfortable—real fast. It is during those times that we are quick to turn to God in prayer asking Him to remove the problem—*PLEASE!*

However, one thing I have learned and that is God will never take us out of our trouble until we allow Him to take the trouble out of us. And once the trouble is removed, God goes on the move through us. In fact, God looks to use our troubles as a passport to bring His state of grace into contact with every person, state or place. This has become more literal for me lately, as I am being blessed with diverse opportunities to speak all over the states—places like California, Nebraska, Boston, New York, Philadelphia, and wherever the call comes from.

> **God will never take us out of our trouble until we allow Him to take the trouble out of us.**

44. THE TRIUMPH OF TROUBLE

Needless to say, it's an honor to be "called" to other places to do God's work. Since my incarceration, the words of Jesus burn in my heart, *"I must be about My Father's business."* And since it is the family business and my Employer owns, ummmm, everything in the world and beyond, I'm pretty sure I'll always have job security under His authority. Not only job security, but longevity and even an eternal pension. You can't compete with such spiritual benefits—*"Blessed be the Lord, Who daily loads us with benefits, the God of our salvation!"* (Psalm 68:19).

Who would have ever imagined that all the pain and adversity in my life would become the catalyst to purpose and ministry? Not many actually. And that is why you only need to know the One who controls it all sovereignly. God knew.

Again, and more bluntly put, God ordains even trouble to be the telescope that brings Him into clearer view for those who are lost in space. Meaning, what gets the attention of the nonbeliever more than anything else? When Gods children suffer successfully, accrediting all peace to God through the tragedy. What else? When circumstances that normally swallow people up like a black hole, actually become the conditions that cause one to shine like a bright star. God uses the holes in our life to allow His light to shine through—the more broken; the more open. Darkness is a prerequisite to seeing the shining stars. *"Those who are wise shall shine like the brightness of the firmament, and those who turn many to righteousness like the stars forever and ever"* (Daniel 12:3).

So if you are going through any of life's afflictions, please know that God desires to bring others to Him through your example of faith as you face the affliction. Consider how the Roman soldier, at the foot of the cross, came to know Jesus was Savior as he uttered these words *"Truly, this was the Son of God"* (Matthew 27:54). What did he see Jesus do? Die? No! He saw Him suffer successfully, as the cross that hung Him became the canvas that magnified Him.

I caused my own trouble, but the trouble I caused is now the ticket that God is willing to use to take His grace and mercy into the hearts of others. I hope that encourages you to bear your pain, don't look to numb it or run from it. For your greatest purpose is discovered in your greatest pain.

45. The Disconnection of Connection

I have always been a people watcher. As a little kid, I remember going to a Phillies game and using the binoculars to scope out the people sitting right behind me in the stands instead of watching the game. My brothers would grab me by my shoulders, tell me I was being rude, and turn me around to face the field.

I haven't changed much since then as my most favorite places to *people watch* are in airports, malls, city streets, and up on the boardwalk where I now live. I am fascinated by the many different idiosyncrasies and personalities that I observe.

Most recently, I was sitting in a mall waiting for my wife to finish shopping and my little hobby once again kicked in. But this time, I found myself thinking about the major cultural shift that has occurred during the five years I was locked away from society.

I now notice a common thread everywhere I go and it runs through all types of people, both young and old. It seems everyone is preoccupied with the same device: the cell phone. It's eyes down and fingers tapping. It's connecting to a virtual community by being totally disconnected to the reality of the people in their presence. There is hardly any interaction, nothing to watch, just people staring blankly into their device: Scrolling and tapping, mindlessly zoned-out.

Don't get me wrong—I saw me in that crowd. I have quickly adapted and been sucked into the "dead-zone" of my iPhone and I feel the strain of having it attached to my hip. I guess it is my love for people watching that has opened my own eyes.

The *bing'ing* sound of my phone has such control over me, because when it beckons me to come by way of notifications, alerts, or reminders, I go without hesitation. And the more I know what's going on within the social media world of my phone, the less I know what's going on within my own personal world. Sadly, my wife and I can be sitting on the same sofa within reach of each other and because of our device and its inviting apps, we can be so out of touch.

So here is my public confession: I am consciously working on disconnecting (or should I say withdrawing—since that is how strong the addiction to this habit really is), as I desire to re-connect with the people around me.

As a youth leader, I can attest that now more than ever before, this generation (which I have previously called the iGENERATION) is the most

> **The world on our phones has made us numb to the world at hand that is right before our eyes.**

45. THE DISCONNECTION OF CONNECTION

technologically connected yet the most spiritually and emotionally disconnected. The world on our phones has made us numb to the world at hand that is right before our eyes.

I can spend more time posting a picture with a thought provoking faith message or Bible verse than actually being that picture in person and living out that verse to the next person. It ought not be.

Am I saying we shouldn't use our handheld devices? No! Use away. But I am saying we should never allow a possession to possess us. Essentially, I can use my phone however and whenever I want, but if it's not benefiting me or blessing those around me, then I need to have the self-control to put it down.

I want to remind us to put away the phone from time to time and take time to "scroll" through Gods Word or "tap" into our families heart. Get personal! Hey, the people around us may not beep when they want our attention, but God designed every soul to crave fellowship with Him and others. It's a given and no app can tell you that.

46. Walking in God-Opened Doors

I recently taught a sermon in my church called "Unashamed: Broken Before God." And before I go any further, I need to pause a moment in awe of the fact that *'I recently taught a sermon in my church!'* It wasn't the first time, but I am blown away by God's grace every time. You see, it is only because of God's faithfulness to make much of Himself through my brokenness that there is even a platform for me to stand on. I am unashamed to claim that.

There's an old saying, "A broken vessel is an open vessel." I not only know that to be true, but I have lived that truth. I am broken and better for it. As I have attested many times before, (in fact now through six years worth of writings), it was the brokenness of my own doing that became the impetus for me to see God so vividly and to hear Him so personally.

I remember when I was in prison and it was inevitable for the question to come up about what I would do in the future. I'm sure many would think my attitude was somewhat delusional because I would boldly state that God had a specific plan for my life and He would bring it to pass in His timing. I would be even more explicit with close family and share the actual vision of what God placed on my heart about my future. I would tell them that I saw myself speaking on multiple platforms—pouring out on others what God had so faithfully poured into me during my time away in isolation.

And since my prison release, I have seen this vision come to fruition, and I will continue to go where God alone has opened the doors. I have been humbled to stand on platforms from Cali to Boston, with many future engagements to come—such as the ACS Music Fest in May, before the Christian band *Mercy Me*, and again this summer at the event, a Closer Walk, held in Wildwood on the beach with the band *Unspoken*.

Another 'God-arranged' engagement will have my wife and I traveling out to Colorado Springs in June to meet with Dr. James Dobson and his ministry team for a radio interview. (I was raised on Dr. Dobson!). Pretty crazy stuff that I know I don't deserve, but I'm realizing God was preparing me for this all along, showing me that the pathway to blessedness must humbly pass through brokenness. The world may throw away what's broken, but God looks to pour into such vessels because they are finally open.

It was through my brokenness that my ears were in tune to another realm as I read the living Word each day and knew that God had a perfect plan for my imperfect life. It was through my broken heart that He began mending and molding His grace into my disgrace. And it was through brokenness that I learned the most about Gods faithfulness.

> **The pathway to blessedness must humbly pass through brokenness.**

The hard truth about life is this: Trials, difficulties, and specifically brokenness are a means by which faith is exercised and increased. God allows adversity as a way for us to get to know Him more deeply. And since mostly everyone can relate to some form of pain, I'm saying that it is usually our hurts that make our platforms most effective as the clearest way to highlight Gods healing. So when trials come and our innermost soul is tested, we shall say:

"I will wait and see what good God will do to me by it, assured He will do it. Thus, we shall bear an honorable testimony before the world, and thus we shall strengthen the hands of others." (George Mueller)

47. Setting the Tone

I am convinced that no matter what happens during my day that my attitude is what sets the tone for me to be bitter or better. My attitude is how people view me and ultimately define me, and it's that disposition that allows others to see what is going on inside of me.

You cannot fake an attitude, nor can your body language hide it. I remember when I was in prison, writing my daily blog, and my mom would report to me that some people commented that my peaceful persona must be me "putting on a good face," in other words, "faking it."

And there were various times in prison where inmates would admit to me that they were waiting for me to show my *real attitude* when things went south. They said it was just a matter of time.

But I knew the importance of setting my 'attitude' each morning when my knees hit the floor renewing my mind on the power of God and His influence on my mindset. And frankly, as time progressed, the inmates realized that you can't fake real.

Attitude is the state of our mind and heart showing through, and our attitudes are usually the first impressions that last—especially when the going gets tough. Too often we allow too many uncontrollable factors to affect our attitude and demeanor.

Instead of having the attitude to overcome the trying circumstances, we automatically settle with the attitude to succumb to trying circumstances. Our attitudes are a choice and nobody can make it for us. It is more important than our accomplishments, our resumes, and even our IQ's.

You can have all the riches and talents in the world, but without a rich attitude that compliments your God-given talents, you actually have nothing. Your attitude is the evidence of what you believe in. If I say, "God is good," my attitude is the proof that validates my words.

Likewise, the attitude that we choose is responsible for our worry or our worship; it affects our emotional stress or success. I am convinced that no matter what obstacle one may face, that attitude is the first thing that must be adjusted in order to adapt and advance.

It is the constant that we control and will speak loudly to those close to us as the outward expression of our inward character. Our attitudes can make us or break us, and especially reveal us; they can progress us or digress us. Our attitudes can be the main reason people become encouraged, inspired, or motivated; and it is the same reason some are disgusted, appalled, or lose heart.

It is very easy to see that our actions are the unfolding of our attitudes.

With all that being said, there are really only four types of attitudes in this world: the attitude that sets the tone, the attitude that is set by the tone, the attitude that watches the tone being set, and the attitude that says, "What tone?"

Which one are you?

> You can have all the riches and talents in the world, but without a rich attitude that compliments your God-given talents, you actually have nothing.

48. Reflect and Reality Check

There is no better day than today to reflect and reality check. There is no better day than today to remember how far you've come and what God has brought you through. Don't focus on how you may not be where you want to be, but reflect on the fact that you are not where you used to be. There is no better day than today.

Along those lines, my father taught my brothers and I, from an early age, the importance of sacrifice and discipline, reflection and progression; whether it was in sports, academics, or just everyday life. He made us understand that we will only get out of life as much as we put in to life, while always emphasizing the importance of honest hard work. He would say with fatherly motivation, *"What did you do today to accomplish your goals?"* Or, *"What can you learn from yesterday to make yourself better today?"*

So as I reflect, then *reality check*, I realize that regardless of where I've been and what I've done, or even where I am now

48. REFLECT AND REALITY CHECK

and what I'm doing, my father only wants my sacrifice and discipline to honor God while always moving forward in faith. Like my Father in heaven, my father on earth loved me in my past mess, and supports me in my present message.

I remember the countless times my father rebuked me for my poor attitude on the soccer field, even after a 5-goal performance. He would quickly remind me that, "it's not about your reputation as a good soccer player (what people see), but it's about your character while playing, whether winning or losing," (what God sees).

He made me realize that nothing can substitute for a positive attitude and Christ-like character. Yet I failed over and over again, but today I know exactly where I'm at and how important my character must be, because it is who I truly am and not what people say I am (reputation).

Even further, I remember shortly after my fatal accident, many friends and family were gathered together for a family function, including my pastor and his young children, yet my father wanted it to be known that his family was not going to be the elephant in the room.

> **Nothing can substitute for a positive attitude and Christ-like character.**

He bluntly and honestly stated how shameful and horrific my situation was, but that responsibility and accountability was our family's goal. He made it clearly known that what I did was inexcusable and that I must be punished for it (I agreed), while demonstrating our family's faith in a God who controls everything.

Today, I see that all my pure qualities were directly learned from my father, and regardless of the tragedy I caused, I know that both my Father in heaven and my father on earth will always love me and support me. Happy Father's Day to him and the father's who also encourage their children to learn lessons from reflection and reality checking.

49. The Answer to the World's Confusion

The more we focus on the confusion and corruption of the world around us, the more such corrosion begins to live within us. So many people are looking for answers—*"What's the solution to the world's injustice, violence, and ignorance?"*—while missing the sad reality that all of what is occurring around the world is the direct result of an increasingly godless society.

I said it before and I'll say it again, bigotry of any type is a matter of the heart. We have collectively lost our way. We are no longer "one nation under God," but rather one nation under fog.

"In God We Trust," still printed on our money, is a daily reminder and remnant of our discarded past. Like our dollar, we have lost our value and have moved towards spiritual bankruptcy.

It's not about figuring out what color matters most, because beneath the skin of every man is a colorless ghost. We need to embrace every race and see individuals as souls who need the Good News of Jesus Christ. He offers true equality because everyone is welcome to be adopted by Him as children.

It grieves the heart of God to hear people arguing about "whose lives matter" only to miss the mega truth that to the Creator God, all life matters—Blues and Blacks, and even the baby that's aborted because science ignores the facts.

The Bible declares, *"Blessed is the people whose God is the Lord"*; yet we have become a nation who has pushed God out and then we condescendingly wonder, *where's God at?*

Nonetheless, there is only one answer to a world that's fallen and that's for the Christian to stand up in their calling—which is putting on Christ's love and regarding others above our own selves. And that's not religion, that's the epitome of every good work and taking action.

Let us not forget that it was Christianity that turned the world upside down in a good way.

Integrity. It was Christ whose love transcended ancient world rules and traditions, elevating the status of women and children.

Equality. Women flocked to Him and slaves were welcomed into early church fellowships where slave and owner washed each other's feet. *Unity.* And in the birth of our country, it was Christ's teaching that was the impetus for the establishment of education, orphanages, hospitals, and every other type of humanitarian effort.

Morality. Even our first colleges and universities began as Bible-proclaiming schools. Yes—and shock alert—Harvard

49. THE ANSWER TO THE WORLD'S CONFUSION

and Yale (originally Puritan) and Princeton (originally Presbyterian). Harvard was even named after a Christian minister; Princeton's first year class was taught by Reverend Jonathan Dickinson; Princeton's crest still says, "*Dei sub numine viget*," which is Latin for "Under God she flourishes."

> There is only one answer to a world that's fallen and that's for the Christian to stand up in their calling.

It has been followers of Christ (both Black and White), who risked their lives to eliminate slavery; it was predominantly Christians who operated the Underground Railroads; it was Christians who hid the Jews from Hitler's ruthless armies. Do you see a pattern here?

In other words, true righteous character can only be discovered in a Person, not in religion, principles, programs, or presidents. His name is Jesus and His way is the only answer to the world's confusion and questions.

Spoiler Alert! Peace will never exist in the whole of this land, but with Jesus, peace can still exist in the soul of man and that peace can influence others and eliminate prejudice from the inside out.

50. Failures Aren't the End

I am living proof that failures aren't the end of living, but can serve as the humbling opportunity to begin again. You see, we all fall from time to time, but it's how we respond and recover that determines—not the outcome—but how we come out on the other side. You never really know the outcome in the beginning of an adversity or as you are moving through a tragedy.

But God does.

He knows the outcome of every circumstance and He can choose to guide us around the hardship or the suffering, but often He chooses not to. Why? Because He has a purpose in mind, which would not be fulfilled if He snatched us out of our valley moments. His major purpose is to deepen our faith, so that when we come out on the other side we can highlight His grace.

> **Even from the deepest pit or the darkest hole, God's redemption can reach into and revive any soul.**

So He allows failure, disappointments, and even tragedy; and then uses all of it as a teaching tool to show us first-hand what true grace, mercy, love, and faithfulness looks like. I can attest to the reality of God at my darkest moments—when there was nowhere to look but up—and it was His presence that surrounded me and filled me. And it was through His Holy Spirit that I not only gained comfort, but I can boldly proclaim the reality and intimacy of my God.

And in the words of Job in the Old Testament, one who was called righteous by God Himself, "*My ears had heard of You, but now my eyes have seen you*" (Job 42:5). Job was a man loved by God and yet God allowed him to lose all of his riches, comfort and health, and worse yet, all of his ten children. And it was after all of that where Job acknowledges a new level of intimacy with God. Remarkable.

Think about that.

Whatever you are facing that is holding you down, look up and through Christ find the strength to get up. And it is right there where God's graciousness shows up. And in my situation, even in my shame. Yes, people will try to remind you of what you've done. But that doesn't mean you have to be defined by what you've done. You see, when Jesus died for the world, He assigned us our worth. He covered our pitiful failures with His successful love. He gave us a new start with each fall and a new beginning with each scar. So even from the deepest pit or the darkest hole, God's redemption can reach into and revive any soul.

Therefore, failures don't need to end with shame. Because when you look at the cross, you will see that Jesus put an end to shame. Which means, by God's grace, there is nothing left for you to do but to begin with faith and surrender everything else at His feet.

51. Living in Today's Trust

What do you do when you've found yourself in-between yesterday's tragedy and tomorrow's triumph? I cannot tell you what to do, but please allow me to share what God graced me to do; and hopefully that will be the inspiration you need to get through.

First off, you cannot worry about the time you will spend waiting in-between tragedy and triumph, knowing that God is always working even while we're waiting. You see, when you think too hard about time, time can seriously get in the way and actually feel like it's slowing down. But when you think about the One who holds the time, you begin to add legs to time because there's no such thing as "dead time" when you're operating out of eternal time. The goal is to "be still"—yet still moving, trusting that God will move when it is absolutely best for you.

> In the "time of in-between" that most would call waiting, God's economy desires us to use the in-between time as training.

Next, you cannot dwell on the past, for what's done is done. And if you look back in regret, you will not be able to move forward into grace; because what you do today will surely affect your tomorrow before it has even begun.

Yesterday's tragedy and tomorrow's triumph are certainly interrelated, but it's only in the present where faith can be regulated and your life can be liberated.

Finally, but not entirely, you shouldn't attempt to look too far down the road. I'm not saying don't cast your vision, but I am saying don't let your idea of the vision to cast you. Because when it's all said and done, it may not look like what you envisioned, and if things start to go in a different direction, then your vision must be flexible enough to take on a new perception. For yesterday's tragedy to turn into tomorrow's triumph, it is mandatory to have today's trust. And that's exactly the secret to keep you from past regret and future fret, it's living in present trust.

In the "time of in-between" that most would call waiting, God's economy desires us to use the in-between time as training. And that's what I recommend you do if you ever find yourself in-between yesterday's tragedy and tomorrow's triumph. Live in today's trust!

52. Now That's a Swan Song

Have you ever heard the term "Swan Song?" It refers to the ancient belief that swans sing a beautiful song in the moment just before death, having been silent or not so musical during most of their lifetime. This proverbial saying stemmed from Greek mythology. I find there is some metaphorical truth to this.

It is often in our darkest moments that we have a decision to make regarding our circumstances. *How will we respond?* Because it is inevitable that when we are squeezed, something will come out—will it be a 'song' or simply 'white noise'?

As we come upon the holidays I was moved upon hearing the history of a particular Christmas song favorite. The song: *I Heard the Bells on Christmas Day*, was birthed—interestingly—through a death.

In the summer of 1861, Henry Wadsworth Longfellow's wife, Frances, died tragically in a fire. The first Christmas without her, he wrote in his diary, "How inexpressibly sad are the holidays." In 1863, as the Civil War was dragging on,

Longfellow's son joined the army against his father's wishes and was critically injured. It was during another upcoming painful Christmas that he wrote this song. It begins as a song of desolation, but ends with these words, *"Then pealed the bells more loud and deep: God is not dead nor doth He sleep! The wrong shall fail, the right prevail, with peace on earth, good-will to men."*

Now that's a Swan Song.

Another favorite song of mine is, *It Is Well With My Soul*, penned by prominent Chicago lawyer, Horatio Spafford.

Spafford's life was full of tragic events. He lost his young four-year-old son to Scarlet Fever. Then, the 1871 Great Chicago Fire ruined his massive real estate business, and his losses were compounded by another economic hit in 1873. At that time, he had planned to travel to Europe with his family, but his plans changed suddenly due to an impending business matter.

He sent his family on ahead. While crossing the Atlantic, the ship they were passengers on, the Ville du Havre, sank after a collision with another sea vessel, and all four of Spafford's daughters, ages eleven, nine, five, and two, died. All FOUR!

His wife Anna survived and sent him the now famous telegram, "Saved alone … ". Shortly afterwards, as Spafford traveled to meet his grieving wife, he penned this timeless song at the spot where the fateful collision occurred. The song concludes with these powerful words, *"Whatever my lot, Thou has taught me to say, 'It is well, it is well with my soul.'*

Now that's a Swan Song.

52. NOW THAT'S A SWAN SONG

As we approach the holidays and New Year, I can only testify from my own life, that whatever burdens are weighing you down—past, present, or future—no matter how dark or hopeless it may appear, that when we surrender our circumstances into God's hands, He will put a Swan's song into our heart. And in spite of the sadness, disappointment, or any derailed dream, our response can be the very song that will lift someone else's burden from white noise to beautiful music.

53. Getting a Hold on Sorrow

This is to encourage all those who are in the throngs of deep suffering. Never forget in the midst of your sorrows, tragedies, and disappointments, that God is right there with you. I know because I wrote this when I was in the throes of my own tragedy. It is my prayer that you will see the flowers of faith that can bloom when we trust and surrender the storms of our lives to Him who sits enthroned above our circumstances.

> *I walked a mile with Pleasure;*
> *She chatted all the way;*
> *But left me none the wiser*
> *For all she had to say.*
> *I walked a mile with Sorrow;*
> *And ne'er a word said she;*
> *But, oh! The things I learned from her,*
> *When Sorrow walked with me.*
> *~ Robert Browning*

53. GETTING A HOLD ON SORROW

What is the prerequisite to plumb the depths of your own soul—sorrow! But only if handled in a godly manner. When you can get a hold on your sorrow and learn to understand 'him', you will begin to learn that 'he' is the plough necessary to uproot wrongly compacted soil and emotions.

Our souls become trodden down over time and left hardened by the resources of life. Until an earthquake erupts, or a trial enters, and tears up the land of our own making, opening up canals and ravines that we never knew existed because the earth of our being was never lifted. For me, I was settled into the dirt of complacency.

Oh how we so need sorrow to better understand joy. Oh how we need to learn how to let sorrows leaves fall gently on our intellect, while raking away the twigs of pity and despair. Those two can have nothing to do with godly sorrow, for they will prolong the landscaping process always putting it off until tomorrow.

I've experienced more clarity in trailing sorrow, following 'his' beaten path to more depth and control over my emotions. I have even found 'his' irrigation in my life to be the very reason there is no more irritation in my life. No longer struggling with releasing my will for God's. No longer responding to life based on the surface survey; rather

> **Never forget in the midst of your sorrows, tragedies, and disappointments, that God is right there with you.**

resting assured that God's resources and minerals are within for my souls purvey. God cannot properly warm me, until I stop wrestling with sorrows blanket. His comfort wants to flood my souls depths to filling, not just sprinkle my feelings.

Therefore, let us ignore the outward commotion, go farther than the shallow emotion, and allow the sorrow of the soul to plunge us into deeper devotion.

"For godly sorrow produces repentance leading to salvation, not to be regretted; but the sorrow of the world produces death. For observe this very thing, that you sorrowed in a godly manner: What diligence it produced in you, what clearing of yourselves, what indignation, what fear, what vehement desire, what zeal, what vindication! In all things you proved yourselves to be clear in this matter" (II Corinthians 7:10-11).

54. Example Trumps Verbal

Call yourself a Christian?

If so, we need to refuse to allow the world to speak louder than us. And when our words won't do it, our walk will. Our peers may not always believe what we say about faith, but it's our responsibility to inspire them to believe by how we act in our faith.

Example always trumps the verbal.

You see, it's easy to recite and spew out the tenets of Christianity, but success comes by living it out for others to see it. Years and years of education, Bible study, and learning theology can be superseded by minutes of humility, honesty, and mercy. You can't get a degree in kingdom thinking. No! This mindset is learned through life's deep experiences—when the going gets tough.

It must be cultivated to be manifested; and often it takes suffering to bring success to the surface.

And that is why God may trust you with trouble: it is His way to show off His grace and glory through the trouble—much like Job in the Old Testament.

> **God doesn't test our present unless He's preparing us for something bigger in the future.**

Job wasn't sinless, just blameless. He walked in his integrity and that was his security. You see, he was secure—not from the devil's external attacks that he suffered—but he was secure by his own internal resilience and reliance on God that allowed for him to suffer successfully through the attacks.

Thus, our security is linked to our integrity.

Yes, trouble touched him, but the trouble did not take him. Job took the trouble and turned it into triumph by his response to the trouble, not by what he knew intellectually—but how he responded to it faithfully. This is abundantly clear in Job's words, *"My ears had heard of You but now my eyes have seen You"* (Job 42:5). It was through Job's adversity that He was able to get a closer more intimate glimpse of the character of God and His faithfulness through our trials.

However, don't be fooled if you have found yourself with no problems, because the absence of trouble doesn't always mean blessing. In fact, the absence of trouble could possibly mean that you are not worthy of the testing. Keep in mind that the devil doesn't mess with those who pose no spiritual threat. Nor does God test our present unless He's preparing us for something bigger in the future.

54. EXAMPLE TRUMPS VERBAL

The truth of the matter is: No one is actively looking for trouble, but if it comes our way, the ultimate goal should be to magnify God through the trouble; because the world is watching and the Christian's example needs to be the steady teaching that should never be lost by a multitude of words and meaningless platitudes that don't line up with our living example.

55. Success of the Soul

I've been doing a lot of thinking lately—maybe because it's graduation season—and since I work with youth, the obvious topic of discussion is *'what are you doing now that school is out or where are you going to college?'*

And I can't help but look back through the window of my own past and have some very strong feelings beginning with the questions: *Is it worth it to gain status and success, yet only to lose your soul through the process?* What you are doing may look like progress, but success alone as the bottom-line can actually be destructive. Progression is commonly looked at as any advancement in life. Diploma. Scholarship. Degrees. Certifications. Promotions. Higher salaries…

I progressed through sixteen years of schooling and obtained a scholarship, which resulted in a degree in Business Administration at Temple University. Progression? Maybe by the world's standards but personally and eternally, not so much. And that is because I was moving up at my soul's expense.

55. SUCCESS OF THE SOUL

The world has us believing that progress is chronologically linked with success. Think about it! "Years involved" in striving to advance only makes one tenured or scholarly or masterly. But if that next stage of "progression" is the ends to the progressive means, I wonder, is the desire to progress controlling you or are you controlling it? I don't know but I know this: Whatever we choose to serve becomes our master—even progression.

> No matter how much one may gain in this world, without Christ, they have nothing. And no matter how much one may lose in this world, with Christ, they have everything.

Outward success does not equal inward progress. So, is there a right type of success and progression? These days I look to a different paradigm to examine that question. Progression can't only mean "chronologically moving forward in success or advancing to another stage of an outward development process." Because if so, how then did Jesus rise well above His contemporaries? How did He progress with His life when it ended up hanging on a cross? At the time, the propagators of theology, royalty, and nobility had ridiculed that He was nothing more than a carpenter; therefore they refused to stop their "progression" and appetite for "succession" to hear Him. They progressed in the world at their souls expense.

Consider this! Jesus was not schooled, nor did He sit at the feet of great Rabbi's. He did not climb the corporate ladder, nor did He spend more than three years in His work. Progression then, had nothing to do with advancing chronologically or succeeding materially and everything to do with developing maturity—success of the soul.

Thus, no matter how much one may gain in this world, without Christ, they have nothing. And no matter how much one may lose in this world, with Christ, they have everything. True progress and success in the soul.

56: Standing Strong

I met a remarkable man at Dr. James Dobson's 'Family Gathering' conference in Colorado Springs. His name is Victor Marx and his life defies all odds. I immediately was struck by his commanding stature, his godly confidence, gentle humility—and all of that—couched within the horror story of his own personal life.

You see, as a child, Victor lived in seventeen houses, and attended fourteen schools. He had four stepfathers. Three molesters. And one unsuccessful attempt by a pedophile to murder him at the tender age of 5, when he was lured into a building, sexually assaulted, and then locked in an industrial cooler to freeze to death. His family found him there, unconscious.

Things didn't fare much better for him in grade school, where a teenage boy began showing him much needed attention with gifts and taking him on trips— this would be classic grooming techniques to ensure his silence when the molestation began. Victor says, "I felt like Humpty Dumpty and I'd fallen off the wall." (Citizen, 2015)

> **Nothing in our lives is ever wasted—no matter how disastrous—when turned over to the Lord.**

How does one survive such gross abuse? Victor's story is so powerful and compelling because it demonstrates how a relationship with Jesus Christ can alter a man and his future. Victor's story exemplifies that nothing in our lives is ever wasted—no matter how disastrous—when turned over to the Lord. It is yet another example of God taking our mess and producing a message. It is what '*Standing Strong*' looks like.

All odds would say that Victor's brokenness as a child would have stunted him, hardened his heart, or perhaps even begun a repeat cycle of abuse on another child. No! Once Victor found Jesus Christ, he allowed Christ to restore and pick up all the broken pieces that within his own human effort was impossible. And out of God's grace and his personal pain, Victor birthed a ministry called "All Things Possible" (ATP).

This ministry has grown exponentially through the years from prison ministry to saving children in conflicts in the Middle East. His heart beats for the hearts of broken children, perhaps because a time long ago, still hidden away in his own heart, he knows well the feelings of neglect, abandonment, and abuse. He has inwardly walked in their shoes.

He continues to impact fractured communities all over the world in Northern Iraq, Syria, Burma, and Cambodia. As a former U.S. Marine and trained martial arts seventh-degree black belt, he teams up with missionaries and has successfully completed six high-risk missions to provide children medicine and support in war torn areas.

The history of this outreach and his personal testimony are chronicled in the film "The Victor Marx Story." And I say all of that to say this: we are in great need of strong, godly men in today's culture. Men like Victor whose lives point to the redemption of the Savior.

57. Sharing the Breath of God

The more I study the Word of God, the faster I come to a humbling realization that I don't know anything about God. And like Job, when His presence is felt, I can only say, "I am a vile person."

Who am I to think I've done anything favorable in my life? Who am I to believe that I am capable of accomplishing on my own ability? Who am I to even attempt to teach other people about God's heart? *"Oh Lord, we are so caught up in our own agendas, that we never stop to consider Yours! Forgive us."*

We falsely think that if we are doing good things and attending church functions that we are in God's will. Meanwhile, the family in the pew right next to us is drowning in pain, yet because we only came to sit in the pew "in Jesus' name," we leave the same way we came in without Jesus' brain. *The mind of God.* His heart would not only attend fellowship, but it would reach out to those around Him who are on the verge of abandoning ship. Their lives are taking on water and their boat is about to capsize. Yet I'm so caught up in my own self-preservation that I

57. SHARING THE BREATH OF GOD

miss the very opportunity to offer someone else the Lord's salvation. I call myself a Christian, but so much I seem to be missing.

The truth be told, if I don't understand the breath of God—which is the Greek meaning of inspiration—I'll never share His breath with another. Not because I don't want to, but because I am incapable of helping anyone else until I understand how Jesus first helped me. Until I grasp the truth that His air is my ever present preservation, not to hold onto for selfish reasons, but to help others through their stormy seasons.

Why do you think the flight attendant on an airplane is so explicit when it comes to instructing the passengers about operating their oxygen masks? Because "in case of an emergency," if you don't know how to safely access the air above that falls from the roofs compartment, then you cannot possibly assist the person in the seat next to you.

That's what inspiration is all about! Receiving and appreciating the breath of God in order to offer His breath to the passenger of life in the seat next to you. In the office next to you. The student in the seat next to you. The family in the next pew.

We think we have life all figured out. But the person who believes that might as well try holding their breath and see how long it takes for them to "let go" of their attempt. We can't even do that on our own, for God is the One who holds the length of our breath in His hands. He gives it to me undeservingly, and if I am a true child of God, I'll learn to share it with others freely.

> **God is the One who holds the length of our breath in His hands.**

58. Take Advantage of the Dash

I heard a really good sermon recently that challenged the listener to consider the impact and legacy of their temporal life. The main question was, 'what are you doing within your dash?' You know, the dash between your birthstone and your gravestone. In other words, what are you doing with your life?

Personally, I have a dash within a dash—if that makes sense. That additional dash was the five-year pause that occurred between the dash of my date of birth (DOB) and my date-of-death (DOD). It encompassed my time in prison—a metaphorical death of sorts—where I was removed from society and reduced to a number 314525E. And though my dashes are all years apart and separate, they are inseparable.

Please let me explain.

You see, every-eternal-thing that God has for me can be fulfilled within that dash from D-O-B to D-O-D (even a pause), the dash represents the time given by G-O-D. I was not responsible for my date of birth, nor am I in control of my date of death. But what I do control are the actions and attitudes that are attached to the dashes latitude.

And while we can micro-manage—to a certain degree—the quality of our lives, it is the time that existed in the dash of my prison life that exposed me to true quality of life. And here's why: I may have been diminished to that dash of time by the system, but what I did *with* the time was not controlled by the system. From arrival to departure, the dash was the most intensive part of my sentence. It was where I learned to truly value time. And though that dash was given to me because of my recklessness, God still used that dash to teach me about His faithfulness. It was in the confines of my aloneness that I experienced God's companionship. It was in the daily chaos that I felt His peace. And it was in spiritual solitude that I heard His still small voice.

A prison Chaplain, Victor Hudson, once said something so simple, yet so profound, and it permeated into my mind and impacted my daily actions. He said, *"Gentlemen, take root where you are planted."* Now I'm not talking about taking on the indoctrination of a prison environment, but rather a spiritual application of utilizing my gifts and talents in spite of the prison walls around me. Take advantage of the dash. So I studied, I led Bible study, I encouraged people, and I shared my resources.

As a result, I am still being blessed by the dividends of the time spent within the dash of my prison life. Those unique experiences, because they were given to me by God's plan, have prepared me for what I am doing today.

So maybe the most important question for you to ponder is: What are you doing with your dash? What legacy are you leaving to those around you? And what are you contributing in this life that will set you up for an inheritance in your eternal destination.

> **Take root where you are planted.**

59. Hold Your Peace

Have you ever felt like you failed miserably in a trying situation? Maybe you lost your temper or spewed out some careless words that you couldn't take back. I know it's happened to me. And oddly enough, it's after processing the circumstances at hand, that I have come to the realization that even in my weakness when things go awry, it can be well worth it if it fosters spiritual growth in me.

You see, I tend to suffer most in the recovery following those moments of failure. I let it play over and over in my mind. I ruminate. But I also trust that the more I suffer because I blew it in my reaction, the more I will eventually have to offer others.

Please allow me to explain.

I allowed a trivial incident to steal my peace in a confrontation with someone and I learned a valuable lesson in the process: I can only be stripped of my peace if I let go of it myself. And let go of it I did—at least temporarily, but long enough to understand that God's peace is something I should never grip loosely. After all, how can I expect to share so willingly something I can lose so easily? I must hold on tighter!

I failed not so much in my actions per say, but in my reaction to someone else disrespecting something I hold dear. Instead of calmly addressing the matter, I responded to the situation in my old nature. I should have taken a breath, uttered a silent prayer, or just covered it in the name of Christ. I quickly realized that giving up my composure and peace because of someone else's irresponsibility makes me the fool.

In I Samuel 10:27, Saul was appointed King and a group of rebels disrespected and despised him for it, refusing to show him the honor and reverence that was rightfully his. We find such a beautiful truth at the end of verse 27, *"But he held his peace."* On such a monumental day for King Saul, in a situation where he had every right to act in force or retaliate, he simply held onto his peace and composure. His response to the rebels' insubordination diffused a potentially volatile situation and kept King Saul's peace safely within his grip.

I have learned that temporary agitations, annoyances, and attacks are just a part of life, but more so, these temporary lapses are helping me realize that my peace will only remain when I intentionally hold onto it through affliction. I may have lost my grip and dropped my peace, but now I know what to watch out for the next time I'm provoked. I thought my grip was strong, but in losing it, I learned how shaky it really is.

Looking back on my life, the people who have always ministered to me the most have been those acquainted with

59. HOLD YOUR PEACE

suffering. There is something so real about them that it makes me feel comfortable being transparent. Suffering comes in all forms, but if we can learn to keep our composure, we will have more to offer in the end. Lesson learned.

"But he held his peace" (I Samuel 10:27)—Humbled to hold on!

60. My Dead Hands

I don't know about you, but for me this is true: I so easily take for granted what God has given me. And it is usually in the process of losing the gift that you finally realize the value of the gift. It has been said "that you don't really know what you've got until it's gone." And I have often said, "whatever you devalue you eventually lose." Now, perhaps you can relate to what I am saying because you have experienced these platitudes from personal experience. Perhaps you have lost something or someone because you took it or them for granted. And perhaps the regret feels permanent or the "thing" lost seems irreplaceable. And it just may be that way.

But God.

You see, when you add God to any situation, equation, or relation, you are throwing off the odds of impossibility and entering into the arena of the miraculous. With God, all things are possible. In other words, no matter the item lost, years wasted, the talent misused, or the person taken for granted, *God can restore the years eaten by the locust* (Joel 2:25). And not only does He restore years, but also, He realigns our heart—so we can better see the gross error of devaluing what is valuable, or in some cases, that which was invaluable.

> When you add God to any situation, equation, or relation, you are throwing off the odds of impossibility and entering into the arena of the miraculous.

For many, it may be too late because that season has passed, or that person is long gone, but nothing is wasteful to a God who is faithful. He takes everything, and I mean everything, and He uses it to re-frame our focus and get us to look more like Jesus. He wants our perspective to be constantly appreciative with what He has given us and He wants our character to take the shape of Jesus.

So how do we do this?

Ultimately, it is when we entrust our lives (and everything attached to our lives) to God's hands that we are trusting His hands to be safer than our best-intended plans. I know all that I am and all that He has given me is better off given back to Him to govern for His glory. But I also know how hard this "casting" back to Him can be. Why? Because I am plagued with the mentality where my focus, without Jesus, is me-centered. And when the "me in me" wins, others always lose.

The Apostle Paul would write, *"I have been crucified with Christ and it is no longer I who live, but Christ who lives in me"*

(Galatians 2:20). And therein lies the loud secret of losing yourself so as to gain God Himself. The "me in me" dies hard however, and declares civil war on soil that is already pioneered by Christ. I know this, yet how many times do I fail to give this struggle to Jesus? Which leaves me taking my life—and everything in my life—back into my own dead hands.

Dead hands cannot grasp the value of that which they hold.

So I pray, *"Lord, I give You my life to hold and I ask for You to give me Your hands to behold this life. Amen."*

61. Isolated Decisions

> **God allows trials to touch us because He loves us and He is unwilling to leave us in the same condition He found us.**

Many people will agree that there isn't a more confused, bipolar month, than the month of March. The familiar saying goes, "March comes in like a lion and goes out like a lamb." For me, the month will always conjure up a pent-up series of emotions that I will live with forever.

It's hard to believe it's been 9 years, since one isolated decision, caused two worlds to implode. Two families caught off guard by tragic news of loss. My recklessness came with a priceless cost. I can't pay it back. I can't take it back. I can't wake up and be back…back where I could make a totally different choice. Back where I can choose not to drink and drive. Those thoughts are delusional, because going backwards is impossible.

Isolated decisions, which take nothing else into consideration except selfishness, always lead to isolation. Isolated emotions. Isolated by pain. Isolated into problems. Or physically isolated by a prison or a program. And selfish decisions in life never *just* affect you. They affect everyone directly or indirectly attached to you. They even infect your reputation and other people's expectations of you.

It's been 9 years since that isolated decision made me an intern to humiliation. My skin still crawls when I think about what I caused, but my spirit remains strong because there is no effect without a cause.

I've made countless decisions since that dreadful night of March 7, 2009, and they too have impacted countless individuals. But they are not isolated decisions anymore that only consider self. They are regulated decisions that consider life over self.

My gauge: How can I infuse life? How can I inspire hope? How can I stand up and influence others toward a moral good? Regardless of circumstances. Regardless of popularity. Regardless of what I've done. How can I live in such a way so as to point to God's only begotten Son?

I'm learning more and more that the true measure of a man or woman is not found in what they do—or even what they've done. The true measure is determined by how they respond to trials in spite of what they do or what's been done. Faith can only be navigated through testing. And hate it or love it, God allows it... because He loves us and He is unwilling to leave us in the same condition He found us.

My heart and prayers remain with the Kap family. *"Thank you for your forgiveness and support."*

Conclusion

I hope these writings have rekindled your faith to see that even in the darkest night that just a spark of light can take over a room. I pray your journey through my months of confinement—and now beyond—give you a new perspective on life. Inspire you to new beginnings.

I am a voice from the tomb of failure sent back to speak life. It is this very failure that was the stench of me and the very fall that buried me. I had to die because of the way that I was living. Dying to the old therefore was the prerequisite to the new.

"It is no longer I who live…" (Galatians 2:20b)

Beneath the surface for a time and it was at that depth that God has allowed me to reach new heights. The grave clothes I wore while writing much of this did not define me. They simply verified that I was a temporary captive from the outside, which only highlighted my liberty on the inside.

These grave clothes are now stripped off and the trajectory of my life has been in full throttle from the emergence of the tomb. I now am a voice from the dead. It's impossible to be contained after your resurrection, especially when you have made it to that point by passing through a spiritual crucifixion. *Unchained.*

"I have been crucified with Christ…" (2:20a).

I may still be criticized, but I cannot be contained. Many may not understand, but that's because they have never met a truly loosed man. Set free from more than the bondage of prison, and more precisely loosed from the carnage of a person. *Self.* My own life was the hindrance to His life, making death the only solution to the problem of me and the very answer of Christ in me.

"It is no longer I who live, but Christ lives in me" (2:20b).

I abhor the thought that I would ever seek to glamorize the tragedy, but I humbly promote the triumph. The voice from the tomb of failure therefore, becomes the evidence of death and the miracle of life. Simultaneously.

"And the life which I now live in the flesh, I live by faith in the Son of God, who loved me and gave Himself for me" (2:20c).

I live because He gave. Life because of death.

Unchained is a choice to be set apart, and these compilations are the manifestation of a voice apart. This conclusion of mine is now your new beginning, and I implore you to use every failure from your past as the evidence that you are a success in Christ. A miracle from God. You are still alive, and your very life is the reality of faith. In Christ therefore, it is possible to turn your tomb experience—death—into a womb of deliverance—life.

Surrender your freedom and become a slave to Christ and realize true freedom.

For *"the word of God is not chained"* (II Timothy 2:9), making free the person who hides God's Word in their heart.

About the Author

Matthew Maher is a 2007 graduate of Temple University, where he earned his Bachelor of Science degree in Business Administration with a concentration in Legal Studies. He is also a former professional soccer player, playing on teams in North Carolina, New Jersey, and Philadelphia respectively.

In addition, Matthew is President of *Soldiers for Faith Ministries* (www.SoldiersForFaith.com), as well as the Teaching Pastor at Coastal Christian Ocean City, where his mission is to inspire conscience (so others may know God deeper) and instigate conviction (so others may make God known wider).

His once admirable life was derailed by a subsequent bad decision that landed him in N.J. State Prison where he served four years and seven months. He was released in August of 2014.

You can learn more at www.TruthOverTrend.com.

Matthew and his beautiful wife, Sarah, reside in Ocean City, NJ. Follow him on Twitter | Instagram | Facebook @TruthOverTrend.

Other book(s) by the Author:

U MAY B THE ONLY BIBLE SOMEBODY READS: R U LEGIBLE?

Imprisoned by Peace: a View Apart.

About the CORE CONVICTION SERIES

You have just read Book #2 of the *Core Convictions Series.* You can find out more information about Book #1, *Imprisoned by Peace*, by going to TruthOverTrend.com. Please be on the look out for additional books in this series, as each unique publication looks to embolden the believer's conviction in Christ.

Matthew Maher says, *"I'd rather stand alone with Jesus than sit in a crowd without Him."*

CONNECT WITH

Matthew Maher

@TRUTHOVER**TREND**

If you are interested in booking Matthew to speak at your next event or would like to check his availability,

VISIT TRUTHOVERTREND.COM

ALSO AVAILABLE FROM
MATTHEW MAHER

U MAY B THE ONLY BIBLE SOMEBODY READS: R U LEGIBLE?
IMPRISONED BY PEACE: A VIEW APART

Thank you for partnering with us in spreading the Gospel
— Matthew Maher

@TRUTHOVERTREND
"spreading the truth in a world of trends"

PUBLISHING

IF YOU ENJOYED THIS BOOK, WILL YOU CONSIDER SHARING THE INFLUENCE WITH OTHERS?

- Share or mention the book on your social media platforms. Use the hashtag #Unchained

- Recommend this book to those in your small group, book club, Bible study, workplace, and classes.

- Share this message on INSTAGRAM, FACEBOOK, or TWITTER: "I recommend reading #Unchained by @TruthOverTrend"

- Pick up a copy for someone you know who would be spiritually challenged and biblically charged by this message.

- Write a book review on amazon.com, bn.com, goodreads.com, or cbd.com

FOR MORE LITERARY INFLUENCE, PLEASE VISIT
www.5511publishing.com

FOLLOW THE AUTHOR ON SOCIAL MEDIA
@TruthOverTrend

Made in the USA
Middletown, DE
18 March 2021